The words we speak are powerful, sha[
us, and consequently our lives. I am [
grandmother's prayer.

I wonder what epic story will play out in the lives of Wyatt and Everly and the rest of my grandchildren yet to be born...

This adventure begins with prayer. Thank you Chris, for telling your story. In doing so, you have reminded all of us of the invitation to participate in the epic story of God's redeeming love. I'm glad I'm a part of it.

## OLIVIA NEWTON-JOHN

Chris played an important role in setting up our first album recorded in the United States. He helped John Farrar find the best studio, musicians, engineer, and the time with Chris and Shanon in Nashville was a short, but wonderful time creating *Don't Stop Believing*.

## KRIS KARDASHIAN JENNER

I remember when Robert came home one day and said he met this guy from Texas. From that day forward, they were both loyal friends until he passed away. The music journey they forged together was a fun, magical time, and the friendship continued when Chris moved to Dallas. Our families had many years of fond memories together during that special time.

These stories are not only interesting, they are examples of the power of prayer. We are blessed to have Chris and Shanon in our lives.

## DANNY WHITE, DALLAS COWBOYS QUARTERBACK

I dreamed of having a hit record. Since a young boy, Chris dreamed of being a Dallas Cowboy. That resulted in a lasting friendship. One of my favorite memories of being a Dallas Cowboys quarterback, was the time Chris and I recorded the "Dallas Cowboy Christmas" albums with the players, Coach Landry and giving back to the community. I'm pleased that those albums are some of the moments in his amazing music journey.

## STAN MOSER, FORMER PRESIDENT OF WORD RECORDS

Chris is a true Christian music legend. When I first heard Chris' amazing music production in 1974, I was determined to find a way to work with him. As the music of the Jesus Movement faded, he was the musical bridge that connected the best pop music melodies and production with life-changing lyrics. He was a true pioneer with his songwriting and production skills that were the driving force behind what we now call *Contemporary Christian Music*—a musical movement that has impacted millions of fans around the world for the last 40 years.

## SAM THOMPSON, ELVIS PRESLEY'S BODYGUARD

I knew Elvis for years as a good friend which eventually led to becoming his bodyguard. There are few people around today that knew, wrote for, and worked with Elvis. Chris and I are fortunate to be two of them.

Having also worked with David Foster and many other music stars, I know how difficult it is to get a major artist to record a songwriter's song. There was no formula for Elvis recording someone's song. The circumstances that led Elvis to record *Love Song of the Year* could only be viewed as a "God Thing". A songwriters first song ever recorded, written in high school, recorded by the King of Rock and Roll.

This book is not just about Chris and his amazing music career, but inside stories about all the other people he has touched and worked with along the way. After many years in the music business, I can't think of a more logical reason the stories in this book would have happened other than the answer to a grandmother's prayer.

## RICKEY STANLEY, ELVIS' HALF-BROTHER

One of the reasons Chris had access to Elvis, was not only because of his music, but because he was a believer. Elvis didn't want to talk about roles in a movie. He wanted to talk about God.

## STEVE ARCHER

It is such an honor to be a small part of this story of the legendary career of Chris Christian! After a decade with my family group *The Archers*, I was blessed to be able to step out and do some solo recordings, and boy did I make the right choice in accepting Chris's invitation to join Home Sweet Home records as a recording artist!

There are so many highlights in the many projects I did with Chris! One of them definitely has to be my recording of the song *Safe* as a duet with the amazing Marilyn McCoo! This recording shows Chris Christian's amazing ability as a producer! Being an artist and songwriter himself, he has an inside track and an amazing ear for great songs, arrangements and just the right people; artist, engineers, and top-notch musicians to bring it all together! Now imagine that many many times over and you're going to enjoy this story immensely! Thank you, Chris Christian, for everything and for including me!

## MARILYN McCOO, RECORDING ARTIST, 5TH DIMENSION

The first time I met Chris was when he appeared on Solid Gold performing his hit. Little did I know it would lead to working with him on two Christian records that would reach #1, and having the opportunity to meet and work with Steve Archer, a beautiful brother in the Lord. From the first time Chris played for me "The Me Nobody Knows," he always believed it would be a major success in the Christian market. He was right. The message was so powerful and a wonderful witness for me to share my faith. It also earned a Grammy nomination in the Contemporary Christian category that year. We also recorded a Christmas project together that continues to get airplay.

## JOHN STYLL, FOUNDER OF CCM MAGAZINE

Chris was first a producer, then an artist, and I feel like the artist image is what stuck. He was also just sort of a general mogul behind the scenes, moving the levers that made everything work, somehow.

## NATHAN EAST, ONE OF THE MOST RECORDED BASS PLAYERS IN THE HISTORY OF MUSIC, SONGWRITER, FOUNDING MEMBER OF FOURPLAY

I met Chris in the early 1980s at his beautiful recording studio in Los Angeles. He was one of the first producers to have a home studio. His approach to making records felt very spiritually guided and we hit it off right away. We worked on numerous projects over the years together most recently a Christmas album featuring the late Natalie Cole & Al Jarreau, the Pointer Sisters, Patti Austin & my group Fourplay among others. I also had the pleasure of working on several productions at his amazing facility The Studios at Las Colinas in Texas including rehearsing with Eric Clapton for the inaugural Crossroads Festival. It's so miraculous how the Lord works through us via the talents we have been given and I will be forever grateful for my friendship with Chris and the blessings of a Grandmother's Prayer!

## KENNY PASSARELLI: AMERICAN BASS GUITARIST, FOUNDING MEMBER OF BARNSTORM*

I met Chris on a plane to Denver from NYC. I was playing Bass, touring and recording with Daryl Hall and John Oates at the time. Just recently ending my 1983 concert, and two albums with Elton John.

We really were from different worlds! We became fast friends. Chris is a visionary and one of the most talented guys I've ever met!! Lots of love to him.

* *Kenny Passarelli also co-wrote: "Rocky Mountain Way". Played with Joe Walsh, Elton John, Dan Fogelberg, Crosby, Stills, and Nash, Stephen Stills, and Hall and Oates.*

---

## GREG MCDONALD: ELVIS AND THE COLONEL'S FRIEND AND BUSINESS ASSOCIATE

I met Elvis at age 10, while cleaning his A/C filter. He introduced me to Colonel Parker and I worked for him until he passed away. I guess I'm still working for him as the manager of his estate.

I met Chris in the early 70's on an Elvis tour. Our paths crossed many times during the Elvis days as well as the time Chris came to meet Lou Pearlman when I was running Lou's companies.

We still get together often, and there are so many Elvis and Pearlman stories we shared together, it always fun to remember them.

I've watched Chris' career for 40 years and I'm grateful the answer to his Grandmother's prayer included our time together.

---

## CHERYL LADD

I shared some great music moments with Chris in California years ago. A real talent with a real heart and a real story.

I had good fun singing on his hit record, 'I Want You I Need You' and got a kick out of watching my husband Brian Russell writing 'Lesson In The Leavin' with Chris.

## BILL GAITHER: SINGER/SONGWRITER, PART OF THE BILL GAITHER TRIO AND THE GAITHER VOCAL BAND

Chris Christian has touched a real nerve: the importance of grandparents and their wisdom and prayers in "bringing up a child." The world and this current culture are simply too difficult to go it alone.

So, grandparents, God is not done with you yet; there is still work to do, and if you have exhausted everything else, those grandkids need your love and prayers. May this book give you some tools to accomplish just that.

# A Grandmother's Prayer

## Moments in a Music Life

## By Chris Christian
with Bill Ireland

True Potential
REACH THE WORLD

Copyright © 2018 CC Entertainment LLC.
P O Box 7809
Dallas, Texas 75209
YMCProductionsLLC@gmail.com

**A GRANDMOTHER'S PRAYER**
Moments in a Music Life

Cover and Interior Page design by True Potential, Inc.

ISBN: 978-1-948794-34-3 (hardcover)
ISBN: 978-1-948794-35-0 (ebook)

Library of Congress Control Number: 2018966498

True Potential, Inc.
PO Box 904, Travelers Rest, SC 29690
www.truepotentialmedia.com

Produced and Printed in the United States of America.

# Dedication

Why Shanon dated me, married me, and stayed with me will always be a mystery to me. She took a guy working at Shakey's pizza, a banjo player at Opryland with a pink bow tie and a straw hat, and somehow decided "That's what I want to spend the rest of my life with."

We could not be more different. I was goal oriented, driven, and not too aware of people's feelings, or mine for that matter. Shanon was not goal oriented, not driven and was the best listener and friend anyone could have.

It is about time I put my cute, skinny legged, tan, long dark hair, sweeper at Opryland, my wife Shanon, at the front of the line after 40 years of asking her to take a back seat to the urgent or the current opportunity. She's seen it all, slept through loud drums or speakers in the basement or a piano in the living room, and who knows what else. Seriously, the odds were not good for us to stay together. But as many times as I ask her "What were you thinking?" she has always said, "I prayed about it, and the Lord told me to pick you and stay with you."

She was even warned by her Dad that she might not be first in my life, and as she said, "I knew he might have been right, but I could not imagine not being along for the ride."

She had no interest in what I did in music, and only cared about the people I had invited to stay with us or became friends with. She's a listener at heart. While I was making music, she was having a heart to heart visit with someone we met or were around. She is the best part of our partnership by far. She was a true apprentice of my grandmother, and has taken my grandmother's love, class, and prayers to another level.

Shanon had a number of years to get to know my grandmother while we were dating and after we were married. My grandmother was the first person Shanon had heard use scriptures as a normal part of her daily conversation. I think it is more than appropriate to dedicate this book to Shanon who daily carries the legacy of my grandmother to our own grandchildren. My grandmother and my wife, those two have few peers that I know.

Thank you Shanon for being a constant rock, a sounding board, and staying by my side when my priorities were upside down.

**Dedicating this book to you is one of the few times I got it right.**

# Contents

Please visit www.grandmothersprayer.com for additional resources, more images, the backstory behind the color images in this book, and to share your "Grandmother's Prayer" story.

# Foreword by Pat Boone

I'm the oldest of 4 kids, born to Margaret Virginia Pritchard Boone and Archie Boone, some 84 years ago. I have a brother Nick and 2 sisters, Margie and Judy, and we all grew up out on Loan Oak Road in Nashville, TN. Daddy was a junior partner and then owner of the Boone Contracting Company, first building homes and repairs for other people's homes and then graduating to building schools and churches - for which my brother and I sometimes dug ditches and poured concrete, pushing wheel barrels 8 or 9 hours a day to try to beat the rain that was coming.

What I'm saying is, we were a rather normal, lower middle-class family. We didn't have a car till I was in the 8th grade, just a company truck, a pickup in which my Dad put a bench he made himself in the back for my brother and me to ride to church and to school - except on rainy days when all 6 of us crowded into the cab.

Lots of funny things, lots of happiness, always food on the table and friends welcome - and we were at church service every Sunday morning, every Sunday night and Wednesday night prayer meetings, and as a family we had devotionals reading the Bible most mornings or nights rarely skipping a day. Even with all of my Dad's work as a building contractor he taught Sunday school on Sunday mornings at the Church of Christ on the David Lipscomb College campus. He took it so seriously that he got up at 6 in the morning to study 6 days a week for a 45-minute class on Sunday morning.

So, the Bible and our relationship with God was just as important to us as food on the table, or our schooling, or occasional happy family outings.

I could sing, but so could my brother Nick, and my 2 sisters. I didn't consider there being anything special about my singing, but I enjoyed it, and I wasn't bashful and would sing whenever anybody asked me to. Nick often joined me, and I thought he was at least as good, if not better, than I was.

But somehow - and this is the main point - I entered a talent contest, the forerunner of American Idol, called Ted Mack's Amateur Hour. That led to a recording contract, and at age 20, I was recording record after record, hit after hit. I had a major recording career that also led to a career in movies and television!

It didn't happen to my brother or my sisters. And through the years, I kept wondering why. Why was I singled out for these incredible blessings? I was very glad, because it helped me to be a blessing to my brother and sisters through the years as well, and they were always so supportive and proud of their "big brother". But I kept asking, why me?

One day I was reading in the Bible about barren Hannah asking the prophet Eli to pray for her because she couldn't have a child. Eli told her, "A year from now you'll have a son" - and she did! It was a miracle of God.

Hannah, (and this is what moves me so much), dedicated that little boy, Samuel, to the Lord holding him up in her arms and saying, "Lord God, he's yours. Thank you that I can raise him, but you use him for your purposes". And God made him the esteemed and revered prophet Samuel. I won't go into all his exploits, you can read those in the Bible, but that incident stuck in my mind.

I asked my mama, finally after some years, "Did you ever do anything like that with me, mama?" She teared up and said, "Yes son, I never told you, but when I brought you home from the hospital I was so grateful to have a healthy little boy like you, that I held you up in my arms toward heaven and asked God to use you for his purposes and to bless you, like he did little Samuel".

Well - we had a good cry together then, and I cry now telling you. What I hope is that other parents and grandparents will lift their children, one by one to the Lord and ask him to bless them as Hannah did little Samuel. Who knows what he may do for your child if you trust that child to Him. Find out.

Foreword by Pat Boone

As two average boys from ordinary towns who simply loved God and music, Chris and I both have been overly blessed. We've had so many things happen to us that really should not have happened--except for a mother's and a grandmother's prayer.

*Pat Boone*

# Acknowledgments

As each album was completed, I always had the privilege to thank people on the album cover that had contributed to making the body of work. I was always thankful to so many that played a role in the project but always very nervous about making a list knowing I might leave someone out.

In the case of those who helped create the music, stories and memories in this book, I am sure I will miss many due to lack of memory, my dyslexia, or who knows why, but I also know to not thank those I can recall would simply not be right. So here goes and please reach out to me if I forgot you, my bad, I'm sorry.

My deepest thanks to everyone who took time to listen, gave me a chance, encouraged me, gave me a job, corrected me when needed, believed in me when there was not a visible reason to do so, and gave me love, help and friendship, which is what life is all about.

## Family Thank You's

JE and June Smith, Mayme and WR Smith, Lola Fry, Neil Fry, Courtney Smith, Casey Christian, Preston and Katie Leigh Smith, Savannah and Justin Andrews, Asher Smith, Caleb Smith, Hollis River Andrews, Landry Smith, Lester and Kathryn Smith, Lacey Scully, and Rachel McCaskill.

## Career Thank You's

Pat Boone, Mike Curb, Elvis Presley, Sherrill Nielsen, Chet Atkins, Jerry Reed, Archie Campbell, Amy Grant, Bob Gaudio, Robert Kardashian, Olivia Newton-John, John Farrar, BJ Thomas, Wayne Newton, Stan Moser, Neil Bogart, Russ Regan, Irving Azoff, Dick Clark, Bob Banner, Bob Siner, Neil Joseph, Bob McKenzie, Don Williams, David Edmondson, Mark Hill, Ross Perot Jr., Danny White, Tom Landry, Roger Staubach, Bob Bruenig, Lance Barrow, Kyle Lehning, David Foster, John Haywood, Bill Cameron, Adam Silver, Mark Tatum, Mark Cuban, JC Crowley, Steve Kipner, Kerry Chater, Gary Paxton, Steve Brack, Leeds Levy, Francis Preston, Robbie Patton, Roger

Sovine, Connie Bradley, Jeannie C. Riley, Tim Robertson, Ray Walker, Charlie Monk, Merlin Littlefield, Michael Gorfaine, Jim Ed Norman, Gene Scott, Harry Warner, Dale Bryant, Owen Sloan, Gary Bernstein, Nola Leone, Tom and Suzanne Hayden, John Femrite, Jennifer Helsley, Todd Baird, Scott Henvey, Matt Crouch, Jeff Crilley, Steve Spillman, Norbert Putnam.

## Friendship Thank You's

Brown Bannister, Robert Kardashian, Kris Kardashian Jenner, Tony Brown, Larry Gatlin, Mark Hill, Randy Nicholson, Joe Leach, Bob Hunter, Kathie Lee Gifford, Ty Miller, John Styll, Burton and Gloria Grant, Dan Harrell, Chris Dunn, Lee Paul, Doyle and Ranelle Gaw, Jeff Williams, Ronnie Price, Trey Yelverton, Debby Boone and Gabriel Ferrer, Kenny Passarelli, Dan Cathy, Bruce Redditt, Trammel S. Crow, Jay Gaw, Lauren Balman, Doug Corbin, Steve Reinemund, Bob Buford, Jim Beckett, Albert Black, Jim Turner, Jerry Durant, Robin Wantland, Tucker Bridwell, Scott Dueser, Dean Bass, Paul Palmer, Rodney Stone, Bob Higley, Carlos Ratliff, Fuzzy Lunsford, Dow Patterson.

## Musicians

**NASHVILLE:** Larrie Londin, Kyle Lehning, Dann Huff, Jerry Carrigan, Roger Hawkins, Steve Gibson, Reggie Young, Joe Osborn, Jon Goin, Johnny Christopher, Bobby Ogden, Shane Keister, David Briggs, Keith Thomas, Bobby Woods, Roger Hawkins, Joe Leach, Steve Schaffer, Bergin White, Harlan Rogers, Mike Brignardello, Hadley Hockensmith, Kenny Buttrey, Johnny Gimble, Weldon Myrick, Terry McMillion, Kurt Howell, Dan Cultrona, Ollie Mitchell, Charles Davis, Peter Brewer, Herb Jameson, Bud Guin, Bob Soma, Joe Ninowski, Collyer Spreen, Ron Jones, Rob Watson, Mark Gersmehl, Gary Lunn, Billy Smiley, Phil Naish, David Huff, Bill Deaton, Kenny Malone, Jack Williams, Ferrell Morris, Pete Bordonali, Dennis Solee, Shelly Kurland Strings, Don Sheffield, Billy Puett, Buddy Skipper, John Carey, Jeff Balding, Jimmy Burch, **BROWN BANNISTER.**

**LOS ANGELES:** Humberto Gatica, Jack Puig, Bob Gaudio, Nathan East, David Hungate, Gerry Beckley, The Archers, Michael Johnson, Kurt Whalum, Paul Leim, Rickey Lawson, Greg Mathieson, Carlos Vega, Nigel Olsen, Michael Landau, Dann Huff, Paul Jackson Jr.,

Christopher Cross, Robbie Buchannan, Cheryl Ladd, Frankie Valli, Bill Champlin, Tommy Funderburk, Robbie Patton, Michael Boddicker, Hal Blaine, Michael Omartian, Paulinho De Costa, Dennis Belfield, David Huff, Jimmy Haskell, Tom Kelly, Bergen White, Tom Scott, Debby Boone, Sandie Hall, Rick Riso, Alex Acuna, Mike Baird, Al Perkins, Abe Laboriel, Tony D'amico.

# The Prayer that Changed Everything

*"And Lord, please let little Chris go into all the world and preach your gospel. Amen."*

As my family members opened their eyes and began to pass the biscuits, I was still lingering on my grandmother's words. I'd heard them before—nearly every time she prayed, in fact. But something troubled me. Was I really supposed to go into *all* the world? In my childish understanding, it seemed like an impossible task. The world was so big! England, Italy, France, Germany, Russia, and a lot of other countries I couldn't even name. Meanwhile, I could barely imagine going to the other side of Abilene, Texas.

Yet there it was in the Bible: "Go ye into all the world and preach the gospel to every creature." It was clearly God's will. **So, if I couldn't go into *all* the world—would I still go to heaven?** These things weighed heavily on me as a young boy, in ways my grandmother couldn't have imagined. Mayme Christian Smith was not just a devout Christian, but a powerful minister as well. We knew her as "Monkey," and my grandfather, who was also a preacher, was nicknamed "Tid." Together they traveled far and wide sharing the gospel. Monkey taught Bible classes for women and wrote books that were distributed all over the country. This was part of the spiritual inheritance I received from my family, which has stayed with me throughout my life.

Our whole family was loving and supportive, but I was closest to my grandmother. To this day, along with my wife Shanon, she's the godliest woman I've ever known. I wouldn't grasp the significance of her prayers until years later. She didn't know how God would answer them and I certainly didn't. But God did. He had a plan in mind that would take me from my quiet Texas home to the center of the pop music world. There I'd work with such established stars as Elvis Presley, Olivia Newton-John, BJ Thomas, the Carpenters, Pat Boone, Wayne Newton, Little River Band, Debbie Boone, America, B.W. Stevenson, All-4-One, the Pointer Sisters, Christopher Cross, Marilyn McCoo, Natalie Cole, Al Jarreau, Amy Holland, Andrae' Crouch, FourPlay, Cheryl Ladd, Kirk Whalum, Austin Roberts, Little Anthony, Billy Joe Royal, and Patti Austin.

In addition to pop stars, God allowed me to work with many wonderful Christian artists, helping to launch or further their careers—Amy Grant, Eric Champion, Dogwood, White Heart, Mark Heard, the Imperials, David Meece, Steve Archer, The Boones, Dan Peek, Honeytree, Rick Riso, Luke Garrett, David Martin, Fireworks, Marty McCall, and Bill Gaither. Along the way, those artists and I had a part in creating a whole new musical genre—Christian pop, or, as John Styll of CCM magazine named it later, *Contemporary Christian Music*.

But that's getting ahead of the story. To tell it right, we need to go back to the 1950s and a peaceful town in central Texas ...

## A Godly Inheritance

Mayme Christian came from a very prominent family in Ennis, Texas, and grew up with the nicest of everything. Her father, Lon Christian, was a successful, self-made cotton farmer. By contrast, my grandfather, W.R. Smith, began life dirt-poor in a tiny house he shared with nine siblings. When he started courting Mayme he was setting his sights high. But they went on to have a long, successful marriage, bound together by their strong faith.

And my grandfather did well himself, becoming superintendent of schools in Clay County, one of the founders of the First State Bank in Abilene, Texas, and, later, vice president of Abilene Christian College (now Abilene Christian University). He was also a respected preacher, delivering sermons every Sunday at the Church of Christ on Eleventh and Willis, just down the street from our house in Abilene. Sometimes when my grandparents weren't out of town speaking, they took me to the church on Saturdays. And there, with my parents and grandparents in the pews, they'd let me pretend to lead the singing and serve communion, as I had seen it done every Sunday. I guess that was my first experience of being on a platform. I wasn't exactly going into all the world yet, but at least it was the other side of Abilene.

For some reason, I liked being at Monkey's house best.

Sometimes I rode my bike across town to her home without telling my parents. They would worry that I was missing—till Monkey would call them and say, "He's here!" One day I packed a little suitcase and walked out to the corner on Willis Street where the busses stopped. I got on the bus—without telling my folks—and somehow arrived at Monkey and Tid's a little while later. To this day I'm not sure how that worked out. It must have been a sympathetic bus driver. Again, Monkey had to call my folks and tell them I was there. Abilene was a safe town in those days. Sadly, I cannot imagine a small child doing that today.

Monkey and Tid's house was on College Drive near Abilene Christian College. It had an evaporative cooler in the window that blew cool air into the room. I can still remember the loud noise of that revolving metal blower. I'd lie on the couch and talk with my grand-  parents over the sound of that cooler, which sounded like a hurricane. To this day, I keep a loud box fan in every room. And I can't go to sleep in a hotel room unless there's a fan blowing. It seems those childhood memories have a lasting impact!

Tid was an incurable jokester. One of his favorite gags was pulling out some plastic dog poop, which he'd place on the floor and then ask me to clean it up. I played along. "Tid," I'd say, "I can't do that. It's stinky!" Tid also had a collection of his favorite jokes, which were written on index cards that he kept in his top drawer. When I was there he pulled them out and tried them on me. The same jokes. Every time I came over.

Nowadays, Tid would probably be diagnosed with Alzheimer's disease or some other form of dementia. But looking back, I find it most interesting and touching to recall how Monkey responded to him. She never scolded him or pointed out that he'd already shared those jokes before. And she never showed a hint of disrespect. She was simply a kind woman who considered it her honor to take care of this man. Now, I'm about the same age as Tid was then, so I can really appreciate how kind and supportive she was.

Monkey was a great cook, and as far as I was concerned her best dish was chicken and dumplings. She'd let me roll the dumplings in the kitchen with a wooden roller. And of course, I always took a few strips of raw dough and ate it before she had a chance to cook it. She also made great grits—with loads of real butter. They turned dark yellow. Mmmmm. Grits are still my favorite breakfast.

This was the world I came into in the early 1950s—a world where strong families were the norm and faith was everything. I was named Lon Christian Smith after Monkey's dad, my great-grandfather.

My grandmother, along with her prayers, imparted to me a strong confidence that never left: *You can become anything you want to become. You can do anything you want to do.* That belief would serve me well through all my wild and unpredictable adventures.

My mother, June—or *Nun-Bug*, as we called her—was just as supportive and constantly echoed my grandmother's words. Encouragement was her middle name. When I started playing music, Mom was my biggest fan. She was the sweetest, most loving mother anyone could ask for.

With all that encouragement, I never felt there were limits on what I could accomplish. And I never saw walls. That became stunningly clear to my parents on one occasion when we visited Washington D.C. While we were there touring the Capitol Building, my parents looked around and suddenly realized I was gone. Then they glanced down on the Senate floor and there I was—talking with Vice President Hubert Humphrey. I had recognized him as an important person, so I wanted to meet him. I realize now that most people wouldn't have done something so bold. But it didn't occur to me that I should feel intimidated. And that attitude stayed with me throughout my life.

## Music without Instruments

In the Church of Christ, we were taught to follow the New Testament in the Bible exactly as it's written. So, if it doesn't say *worship the Lord with a guitar in your hand*, then you'd better not do that. That's why the Church of Christ had no musical instruments in their worship services.

But we did *sing*. Everyone would try their best to pick out one of the four harmony parts written in the hymnal. *What a Friend We Have in Jesus. Fairest Lord Jesus. A Mighty Fortress is Our God. Trust and Obey.* Those old hymns are all emblazoned in my memory. To me, that *a cappella* singing was boring, and about as pleasant as hearing fingernails on a chalkboard. But it also sparked my musical imagination. While others were following the notes in the hymnal, I heard different, more elaborate arrangements in my head, with all kinds of instruments. That tendency continued and eventually led to my career as a record producer. I could listen to a primitive song by an unpolished artist—and hear what it *could* be.

In a supreme irony, many of the musical colleagues I worked with later also came from the Church of Christ. When we get together, we often remark how amazing it is that so many great Christian musical careers arose out of a church that prohibited musical instruments! That underscores another theme I've noticed through the years: Our God is too big to fit into any box. In fact, there are no boxes ...

## Life in Abilene

In grade school, our football team had two plays. Play One: the backfield would line up on the left and then the quarterback, which was me, would run left. Play Two: the backfield would line up on the right and I ran right.

Every now and then, we switched things around just to confuse the other team. The backfield would line up on the right and I ran left. Either way, I was fast enough that they could never catch me. During sixth grade, we won every game and the city championship.

Things usually seemed to work out well for me. I became accustomed to winning, whether it was a football championship or a blue ribbon at the science fair. Some people might say I was just lucky or talented or was benefitting from some special advantage. But I knew better. I had a secret—I was always praying. My grandmother had taught me that God answers prayer. And I believed it. So, in my childish way, I simply asked God for the things I desperately wanted, and often I received them. Those things may seem trivial now, but at the time they were all-important. God and I were a team; we had a thing going. I was to love, trust and obey Him. And He would take care of me and make sure I got what I needed.

I was always a blue jeans and T-shirt kind of kid. But as supportive as my mom was, she hated blue jeans. She always dressed impeccably herself. "I never go anywhere before I put on my face," she used to say. The casual style of kids in the '50s just rubbed her the wrong way. I was notorious for never making my bed. So, when I brought a pair of blue jeans home one day, she hid them in the one place she knew I would never look for them—under the tangle of sheets on my bed.

That was life in Abilene during the 1950s.
Childhood was simple, challenging and
fun. There were science fairs and talent
shows; Boy Scout camps, baseball, football and basketball. And I enjoyed all of
it. I was on track to live a good, successful, but ordinary life in my hometown.
Someday, I would probably go to work at
the bank my grandfather had founded,
as my mother and father had. And that would be just fine.

But when I was in fourth grade, something came out of the blue that
changed it all. And from that moment, I knew what I wanted to do
with my life.

# 2

# I Heard It on the Radio

It was a day like any other as I got ready to go to my fourth-grade class at Crockett Elementary School. Little did I know that this day would set my path, changing my life and the lives of so many others.

Mrs. Patterson was our teacher, and if you believe in coincidences (which I don't) she had a son who was a popular musician in Abilene. Dow Patterson had a hit song on our local radio station. For all I knew, it was probably a hit everywhere in the world. I didn't realize yet that there were radio stations like ours in every city across the country that would play their local talent. To everyone in Abilene, Dow was a big star.

Around this time, rock and roll was in its prime and young people everywhere were obsessed with Elvis Presley. So Dow, with his acoustic guitar and appealing style, fit the current image just right. Imagine— here was a famous singer in our town, and his mom just happened to be my teacher. Incredible!

Even as a young boy, I was never afraid to approach people and ask questions. So one day after class I walked up to my teacher and said, "Mrs. Patterson, could you ask your son Dow to come and sing his hit song for our class?" It didn't occur to me that big stars don't usually perform for fourth-graders. But amazingly, she said yes. And a few days later, there he was—Dow Patterson himself at Crockett Elementary, singing for our whole class. As I watched him perform *Gena* on Winston Records, I said to myself, *That's what I want to do!*

After Dow's performance I approached him and began asking questions. What was it like being a big-time musician? How had he managed to get a record on the radio? What advice would he give to someone who wanted to do the same thing? Dow was very patient and helpful, and even signed a photo for me: *"To Chris—Best wishes and loads of success with your music! Dow Patterson."* Only years later did I appreciate how unusual it was that he would write such words to a young child. Not many kids know what they want to be by the fourth grade. But I guess my enthusiasm convinced him that I was serious. Anyway, his encouragement meant a lot to me.

My path was clear. I would become a songwriter, singer and musician like Dow. And I started preparing right away. I wrote my first song while I was still in fourth grade, and can still remember the lyrics:

*The clouds are high in the sky*
*The dark clouds are going away*
*And the white clouds are coming to stay.*
*It's going to be a nice day!*

The first instrument I could get my hands on was a Harmony ukulele. In fact, it was the only instrument with a neck my fourth-grade hands could fit around. I taught myself to play it, and by the end of sixth grade I was on stage performing for the student body with my friend William Lamar. The next year he and I formed a group with Steve McMillon, who played guitar. We called ourselves The Drifters, not knowing there was already a famous rhythm and blues group with the same name.

My next goal was to get a guitar. So I began mowing yards and doing odd jobs, anything I could to make money. Finally, I saved enough to buy an Airline guitar at Montgomery Wards. I still have that guitar.

Then, it was on to the piano. My father was J.E. Smith (we called him *Daddy Bear*). I started writing little notes to him and leaving them under his pillow every night: "Daddy, please get me a piano." It eventually worked. My persistence wore him down, and he bought an old upright piano for fifty dollars and put it in my bedroom. That night, my mother and father were eating supper when they started hearing

piano music from somewhere in the house. They came to my bedroom, where I had already worked up some songs. It continued that way night after night—I played the piano every chance I could get. I think it nearly drove my dad nuts, but of course my mother thought it was beautiful. I often heard my dad tell others, "He was just born with music in his bones."

Later, my dad arranged for me to take lessons from a local piano teacher. But my instructor made two mistakes: At the end of each lesson he leaned over me, puffing billows of cigarette smoke in my face. Yuck! He also played the next week's assignment, so I could hear what it was supposed to sound like. But once I heard it, I could always play it right back—no written music needed. After two weeks, I was done with piano lessons.

At my request, Mom would always take me to the Caldwell Music store on weekends. There I looked at all the instruments for sale and played as many as they let me. I looked through the sheet music racks to find out who wrote all those songs I'd been hearing on the radio, and who owned them. Then I asked her to take me to Brown's Hi Fidelity in downtown Abilene, which carried record players, guitar gear, speakers, microphones, and headphones. To me, going to those stores was like a fashion person going to Neiman Marcus.

Mom didn't mind me playing the piano late into the night or setting up drums in the living room and beating them for hours. But no matter what instrument I was playing, she would always put her head in the door and say, "That is so beautiful! What song is that?"

My dream was to write songs, make music, and have it played on the radio, like Dow Patterson. It never entered my mind that music could actually be my career. I figured that was reserved for the folks in the big cities—Nashville, Los Angeles, or New York. After all, no one from Abilene had ever done anything like that. In our town, people generally made a living in oil, real estate, ranching, or banking. Music was simply my hobby. But I gave my heart and soul to it, practicing guitar and piano every day after school, writing songs, and entering local talent shows whenever I could.

## Meeting the Music Pros

As the '60s rolled on, the popular music artists of the day captivated my imagination: the Beatles, Peter, Paul and Mary, the Turtles, Gary Lewis and the Playboys, Paul Revere and the Raiders. And of course, Elvis Presley, the king of rock and roll. Every now and then a big musical act would come to perform in Abilene. I knew instinctively that the best way to advance in what I wanted to do was to meet people who were already doing it. Beyond that, the people who were writing songs, making records and playing their music for crowds simply fascinated me. So, whenever a group came to Abilene I looked for every opportunity to meet and talk with them. I did see Elvis in concert in Abilene, which was amazing. But after the show, Elvis left the building and I didn't get a chance to meet him then. I never dreamed that I *would* meet him eventually—and he would come to play a big role in my life much later.

Around this time one of the hottest acts in the country was The Association. They had a string of top-ten hits, including *Cherish*, *Windy*, *Never My Love*, and *Along Comes Mary*. They came to perform in Abilene when I was in high school and I managed to get a gig driving them around town. I even got to hang out with them in their hotel room.

What a blast! *Along Comes Mary* was recorded in Gary S. Paxton's garage. Gary would give me an opportunity to work with him many years later in Nashville that would lead me to Elvis. I had similar opportunities to meet the groups Blood, Sweat and Tears and Three Dog Night. I also met the 1910 Fruit Gum Company, which had several hits in the "bubblegum" pop genre. They were signed to Buddah Records, a label headed by Neil Bogart. Years later, Neil founded Boardwalk Records— and signed me as that label's first artist. Unusual connections like that, which I could never have orchestrated, would become a theme in my life. Over the years, those intersecting relationships enabled me to bridge different groups, different genres, different times, and different cultures.

One music act that made a huge impact on me was the Carpenters. Their smooth, mellow sound had propelled them to the top of the pop charts with hits like *We've Only Just Begun*, *Top of the World*, and *(They Long to Be) Close to You*. Karen Carpenter had a soothing contralto voice that blended perfectly with her brother Richard's creative arrangements. Their lush vocal harmonies were similar to what I heard in my head when I listened to hymns in the Church of Christ. So right away, I was captivated by the Carpenters. The soft rock style they perfected would eventually evolve into the adult contemporary genre that's still popular today. When I was a student at Abilene Christian College, I heard that they were coming there to perform. So naturally I was excited to hear them. After their concert, I made my way backstage and found their road manager. "Where are y'all going after the show?" I asked him. It turned out they were headed to the restaurant in the local Ramada Inn. So, I hightailed it over there, hoping to spend some time with them. There I met their guitar player, Tony Peluso. I told him I was a musician too and interested in the music life. He was friendly and gracious, answering all my questions as we munched hamburgers together. And by the end of the evening, I felt we were friends. He then introduced me to Karen and Richard. Seeing an opportunity, I told Richard I was a songwriter and would like to send him some of my songs. Before the evening was over he had everyone in the band, including Karen and himself, autograph the back of a placemat for me. And at the bottom, he wrote his address, so I could send him my songs. Recently, I found that placemat again among a bunch of other memorabilia. It's now framed and mounted on my wall next to my Double Platinum Carpenters record.

One of the great thrills of my life came in the 1980s when the Carpenters recorded my song, *(Want You) Back in My Life*—with my friend Tony Peluso playing guitar. It was also a single off the *Coming To America* album and included on the *Yesterday Once More* Double Platinum album. Another example of a connection coming full circle.

But as a young student at Abilene Christian, I couldn't have foreseen all that. In fact, back then I couldn't imagine my music reaching beyond friends and family. But that was about to change in an amazing way.

TOP 50 Adult Contemporary

These are best selling middle-of-the-road singles compiled from radio station air play listed in rank order.

| This Week | Last Week | Weeks on Chart | TITLE, Artist, Label & Number (Dist. Label) (Publisher, Licensee) |
|---|---|---|---|
| 1 | | 9 | SHARE YOUR LOVE WITH ME<br>Kenny Rogers, Liberty 1430 (Duchess, BMI) |
| | 3 | 7 | HERE I AM<br>Air Supply, Arista 0626 (Al Gallico/Turtle, BMI) |
| | 4 | 10 | HARD TO SAY<br>Dan Fogelberg, Epic 14-02488 (Hickory Grove/April/Blackwood, ASCAP) |
| 4 | 2 | 12 | I COULD NEVER MISS YOU<br>Lulu, Alfa 7006 (Abesongs, BMI) |
| 5 | 5 | 11 | ARTHUR'S THEME<br>Christopher Cross, Warner Bros. 49787 (Irving/Woolnough/Unichappell/Begonia, BMI/Hidden Valley, ASCAP) |
| | 7 | 12 | WE'RE IN THIS LOVE TOGETHER<br>Al Jarreau, Warner Bros. 49746 (Blackwood/Magic Castle, BMI) |
| | 12 | 6 | THE OLD SONGS<br>Barry Manilow, Arista 0633 (WB/Upward Spiral, ASCAP) |
| | 8 | 7 | THE THEME FROM HILL STREET BLUES<br>Mike Post, Elektra 47186 (MGM, ASCAP) |
| | 10 | 7 | JUST ONCE<br>Quincy Jones Featuring James Ingram, A&M 2357 (ATV/Mann & Weill, BMI) |
| | 13 | 5 | OH NO<br>Commodores, Motown 1527 (Jobete/Commodores Entertainment, ASCAP) |
| | 11 | 8 | WHEN SHE WAS MY GIRL<br>The Four Tops, Casablanca 2338 (MCA, ASCAP) |
| 12 | 6 | 14 | STEP BY STEP<br>Eddie Rabbitt, Elektra 47174 (Briarpatch/DebDave, BMI) |
| | 17 | 6 | ATLANTA LADY<br>Marty Balin, EMI-America 8093 (Mercury Shoes/Great Pyramid, BMI) |
| 14 | 14 | 7 | BACK IN MY LIFE AGAIN<br>The Carpenters, A&M 2370 (Duchess, MCA/Home Sweet Home, ASCAP) |
| 15 | 15 | 6 | TAKE ME NOW<br>David Gates, Arista 0615 (Kipahulu, ASCAP) |
| | 18 | 8 | IT'S ALL I CAN DO<br>Anne Murray, Capitol 5023 (Chess, ASCAP) |
| | 22 | 3 | WAITING FOR A GIRL LIKE YOU<br>Foreigner, Atlantic 3858 (Somerset/Evensongs, ASCAP) |
| | 21 | 6 | ALIEN<br>Atlanta Rhythm Section, Columbia 18-02471 (Low-Sal, BMI) |
| | 24 | 4 | I WANT YOU I NEED YOU<br>Chris Christian, Boardwalk 7-11-126 (Marvin Gardens/Home Sweet Home/Bug And Bear, ASCAP/John Charles Crowley, BMI) |
| 20 | 23 | 6 | STEAL THE NIGHT<br>Stevie Woods, Cotillion 46018 (Atlantic) (Sunrise, BMI) |
| | 30 | 2 | WHY DO FOOLS FALL IN LOVE<br>Diana Ross, RCA 12349 (Patricia, BMI) |

# 3

# From Small Beginnings

*"Do not despise these small beginnings, for the LORD rejoices to see the work begin ..."* – Zechariah 4:10 (NLT)

It was orientation day at Abilene Christian College. I had made the easy choice to attend the school where my family ties were, not realizing that most people look at several colleges before choosing one. To me, this first year of college at Abilene Christian was like the thirteenth grade of high school. I was sitting on the steps of the administration building wondering what it would be like. Soon I noticed two other guys sitting nearby, who seemed as unfamiliar with the experience as I was. We struck up a conversation and quickly hit it off. One of them was Mike Blanton from the north Texas town of Amarillo. The other was Brown Bannister from Fort Worth. As we talked, I sensed the beginning of a friendship.

We couldn't realize it then, but that seemingly-chance meeting would impact the rest of our lives—and eventually play a role in changing a part of the music industry. But on that September day we were just three young guys hoping to get through college, not get drafted, and do something good with our lives.

Mike, Brown and I became inseparable for the next four years. We were like the Three Musketeers. We even lived together during our junior and senior years. And we shared lots of experiences—some great, some goofy, and some embarrassing. Like all young men, we sometimes felt the urge to sow some wild oats. But in our case, we were so conservative that our sowing was tame, considering the times. One night we sneaked out of our house in our underwear about two a.m., ran three blocks to the college fountain and poured Tide detergent into the water. I can't speak for Mike and Brown, but that was about as wild as I got.

Around midnight after we finished our studies, we started feeling hungry. So, one of us would give the signal: "Squeet!" That was code for *let's go eat*. And off we drove to the Saddle and Sirloin, a local diner across town. There we spent hours talking and sharing dreams with each other, usually topping the night off with lemon ice box pie. Naturally, we hoped to be successful someday and we imagined what that might be like. In one of our fantasies, we decided to open a ski lodge together. Why not? Of course, there was no snow skiing on the plains of central Texas, but it just seemed like a glamorous thing to do. We named our fictional ski resort the *Home Sweet Home Lodge*. We fantasized about calling the pilots of our private planes, telling them, "We'll be at the FBO in an hour!" Then off we'd fly to our Colorado ski lodge.

One night, the images seemed so vivid I almost forgot we were just dreaming. That was quite an imagination for three college guys in Abilene. But our fictional adventures brought us lots of fun and joy. I never forgot those sweet times, when I was so naive and confident. Back then, everything seemed possible. Later when I moved to Nashville and started my first jingle company, you can probably guess what I named it: Home Sweet Home Jingles.

# Chris, Chris and Lee

At that first orientation on the steps of the administration building, the school announced that it would be holding a freshman talent show at the end of the proceedings. Anyone who could sing or play an instrument was welcome to participate. Abilene Christian College was affiliated with the Church of Christ. I've sometimes referred to it as our "Vatican"—it was that important. And as I mentioned, the Church of Christ was famous for not allowing musical instruments. But that restriction only applied to the church worship services. Outside of that, all kinds of music and instruments were okay. I had sung and played my guitar in talent shows since the sixth grade, so this seemed like a natural opportunity for me. There were a couple of other freshmen sitting close to me at orientation, and it turned out they played instruments also. Lee Paul was a banjo player who had spent the previous few summers playing at Six Flags Over Texas, a theme park in Arlington. My other new friend was Chris Dunn, a Church of Christ minister's son from San Antonio who played guitar. We began to talk about putting some songs together. After a few rehearsals and memorizing some

Peter, Paul, and Mary songs, we made our debut at the talent show. It seemed to go over well, and afterward Bob Hunter, the college vice president, came up to talk with us. He had a proposal: If we would agree to play at future alumni events and fundraisers for the college, he would arrange a full scholarship for us. It was an offer we couldn't refuse. I had hoped to try out as a walk-on for the school's basketball team, since I had played basketball at Abilene High School. But playing music a couple of times a week sounded a lot easier, with less chance of injury—not to mention, more fun. We'd get to play music—which we would have done anyway as a hobby—and receive a full ride scholarship at the same time. What an opportunity! That was just one of many ways Bob Hunter helped me through the years, and I'm forever grateful for his kind and generous presence in my life.

Ch 3. From Small Beginnings

In an ironic twist, I found out much later that when my grandfather was vice president of Abilene Christian College, he had once taken a cold call from a young Bob Hunter who said he had no money but wanted to attend the school. So, my grandfather arranged a full scholarship for *him*. That enabled Bob to attend and complete his education at Abilene Christian, serve the school as vice president—and many years later extend the same generosity to me, the grandson of his mentor. The connection had come full circle, by God's grace. Some things are just too amazing to be mere coincidence.

We named our group Chris, Chris and Lee, and became a real, working music act. Along with alumni fundraisers, we played at local venues, covering hits of the day by Bread; Peter, Paul and Mary; Crosby, Stills and Nash.

We even got to tour with Dallas McKennon, who played Cincinnatus on the popular *Daniel Boone* TV Show starring Fess Parker. We opened for him on and off for a year, traveling with him on a private plane. On one trip we were flying to Paris, Texas for a rodeo show. As the plane descended towards the runway, I heard the pilot yell,

"What is that?"!!!!!

Dallas McKennon, "Cincinnatus" of "Daniel Boone" NBC TV Show.

There, in the middle of the runway, was a Caterpillar dirt mover. It turned out, the operator had just stopped his machine and gone to lunch. We had to abort the landing and circle until his lunch break was over! Daniel Boone was a big TV show in those days, so it was quite an honor to tour with Dallas McKennon.

Chris Dunn and I had both written a few original songs and we were eager to record them. That opportunity finally came when my uncle Neil Fry put up the money for our first album. In Abilene there was a man named Mr. Buford who had a two-track reel-to-reel tape recorder in his home. He called it a studio, but it was really just a house with a microphone in the living room and a reel-to-reel tape recorder in the bedroom. This was probably where I got the idea of a home studio. With my uncle's investment, we recorded there and completed an album—in just two days. The recording setup was primitive, but Mr. Buford knew how to make the most of it. He was blind yet had a good music sense and a great ear for sound. I learned a lot

from that experience and wish he could have known how much he taught and helped us. I think he'd be happy to see how our musical paths developed, thanks in part to his encouragement.

Chris Dunn went on to a very successful career as a songwriter and producer in Nashville, writing hits for Tim McGraw, Terri Clark, Tanya Tucker and Cindi Thomson. And his sister, Holly Dunn, became a successful singer-songwriter in her own right during the 1980s.

Chris Dunn adopted his middle name as his last name, so he is known to the world as Chris Waters. My name change came later when I needed to join ASCAP as a songwriter. There was already a Chris Smith registered, so I simply took my middle name, which was my grandmother's maiden name, and became Chris Christian. I would have never picked that name if I had known what type of records I'd be making years later. As you can imagine, I've received a lot of ribbing about that. When I did concerts, I was often greeted with "Hey, *Herbie Hebrew!*" or, "*Willie Witness!*"

I was about to embark on a lifelong musical journey that's still unfolding to this day. But there were some detours I would have to take first. Sometimes discovering what you *don't* want is as important as finding what you *do* want. After that first year in college, I spent the summer working at One Main Place Bank in Dallas. Years later I found out that I got the job because my mom used to date Gilbert McClesky, the bank's vice president. As a delivery guy for the bank, I was handling large sums of money—but not getting paid much myself. The worst part was that I simply found the work terribly boring.

I realized quickly that I was not cut out to be a nine-to-five banker. It had been a great career for my dad, but it was never going to work for me. Dad used to tell his friends, "It's hard to get Chris to work nine to five. But he doesn't mind working twenty hours a day." That was a pretty sharp insight into the way I tick. Thankfully, God was about to reveal a very different plan for me. And it involved a man who would play a pivotal role in my life, time and time again—Pat Boone.

Like many in Abilene, Pat came from the Church of Christ. He had always been a strong supporter of Abilene Christian College and was a good friend of Bob Hunter. Bob liked my music and thought Pat might like it too, so he sent Pat a demo tape of my songs, which I had recorded with Chris, Chris and Lee. To my surprise, and everyone else's, Pat wrote back a few weeks later, saying he really liked a song called *Thank You* and wanted to record it. It would be a few years before that actually happened, but his response right then meant the world to me. Pat Boone was a big star and his endorsement confirmed that my music might have some real value. Pat's letter also caught the attention of another important person close to me—my dad. And the combination of unlikely events was about to propel me into a whole new adventure in pop music.

# 4

# Off to Music City with $100

It was my sophomore year at Abilene Christian College. I told my dad
I needed a job for the summer—thinking he might get me a job at the
bank. But he surprised me. "Pat Boone seems to like your songs," he
said. "Why don't you go see what that music thing is about?" My dad
knew absolutely nothing about the music business. But he knew that
music was what I really loved. And he was wise enough to give me that
nudge, which I never would have thought of on my own. Besides, as
he reminded me, I still had a fallback option if it didn't work out: "You
can always come back and work at the bank."

My dad's encouragement marked an important turning point for me.
If he had not made that suggestion I might never have had a music
career. After all, that wasn't a normal choice for
people like us. Banking had been our family's
business for generations. My granddad, W.R.
Smith, was one of the founders of the First
State Bank in Abilene. My mom was its first
employee, and my dad had followed her into
the family business. Dad spent his life going to
the bank every day at eight a.m., coming home
to lunch for one hour, and returning to work

till five. He did that for forty years. I had no reason to think my life
would be any different—until he spoke those words. Somehow he
knew that, for me, finding my passion was more important than following in his footsteps.

So I packed up my black Chevy station wagon and took off for Nashville. I had $100 my dad had given me and some reel-to-reel tapes I was ready to play for anyone who would listen. I had no idea what I hoped to find, only that I wanted to make music and Nashville was closer than New York or Los Angeles. I had asked Pat Boone if he knew anyone in the music business there who might help me. He gave me the name of Ray Walker, a Church of Christ song leader who had been Pat's roommate in college. Ray was also a member of the Jordanaires—the famous gospel quartet that backed Elvis Presley.

In Nashville I found an apartment across from Belmont College that I could rent for twenty-five dollars a week—rats included. Once I got settled, I walked down Music Row, knocking on the door of every publisher I could find. The response wasn't exactly overwhelming. "I'm sorry, sir," the receptionist would say, "We don't consider unsolicited material." There were two people who did give me some time—the manager at Peer-Southern Publishing and Fred Foster at Monument Studios. I'll always remember their kindness for giving this newcomer a chance to have his songs heard.

Everyone was courteous, but the answer was always no. The few times I actually got to play my songs, they still turned me down. In my naiveté, I just figured they didn't have very good ears. Couldn't they tell that these songs were great? Now that I have a few more years' experience, I'm surprised they didn't burst out laughing—especially as they heard classics like *The Pink Song*, a tune I'd written about a pink giraffe. All songwriters think their songs are great, just as all parents think their children are beautiful. And a song is like a child. I call them "Music Babies". I've learned that there are no ugly music babies—at least in the eyes of their creators.

At Pat's suggestion, I did call Ray Walker. He was very gracious and spent a lot of time with me over several days, explaining the music business and how things worked. I thought I was ready for prime time.

Ray had a more accurate picture and knew I had a long road ahead of me. To this day, I'm grateful for his generosity helping a newbie. Later I learned that I was just one of thousands that Ray Walker helped throughout his career. Even though he couldn't do much except offer encouragement, Ray made me feel that Nashville folks were my kind of people. And that was a great help all by itself.

After two weeks, I'd had no success and my money was running out so I decided I needed to go back home. I called my parents and said, "I'm coming back to Abilene." But once again, my dad came through with a better idea. He mentioned that his friend Bill Marable from Knoxville, who had been his B-52 copilot in World War II, had invited him and my mom to the Chet Atkins Guitar Festival. They weren't able to go, so why didn't I go in their place? It was going to be in Knoxville and, being in Nashville, I was already most of the way there. "Just go to the festival," Dad said. "Then you can come home." It made sense. And it would be one last adventure before I returned to Abilene. I said to myself, *Why Not? What do I have to lose?* So I loaded up my clothes, guitar and tapes. And off I went, again.

## Finding a Way In

In Knoxville I met Bill Marable, who gave me his tickets since he wouldn't be attending the show himself. The Chet Atkins Guitar Festival was where the best guitar pickers from all over came to perform, along with other famous artists. At the arena I was met by an usher who escorted me to my seat. We walked and walked, till we were near the front row—the best seat I could have asked for! Once more, I was up close with musicians who had made it in the business. I could feel my aspirations rising again. But then I remembered that after this, I'd just be heading back to Abilene. So my excitement was tinged with regret.

ENTER NOW . . . 3RD ANNUAL

**CHET ATKINS GUITAR FESTIVAL**

FINALS: APRIL 28 & 29, 1972
KNOXVILLE, TENNESSEE

**DEADLINE FOR ENTRY APRIL 1, 1972**
2 Categories:
★ ELECTRICAL
★ CLASSICAL

COMPETITION LIMITED TO GUITARISTS
Between the Ages of 14 and 23 As Of April 27, 1972.
TO ENTER PRELIMINARY COMPETITION: Submit a 5 Minute, Mono-oral Solo Audition Tape Playing the Composition You Will Play in the Finals, and a Copy of Your Birth Certificate.

Name
Address
City                          State
Telephone                     Age

**CHET ATKINS GUITAR FESTIVAL**
1516 16th AVENUE, SO.        NASHVILLE, TENNESSEE 37212

Toward the end of the show, I noticed that a security guard at the backstage entrance had left his post to talk with someone. I decided to pull a "Hail Mary."

I walked backstage just as if I belonged there. One of the first people I saw was the TV star Archie Campbell. At that time, Archie was a writer and performer on the hit show *Hee Haw* and did comedy performances around the country. I knew that Archie's son Phil attended Lipscomb College in Nashville—another Church of Christ school where I'd been thinking of taking a summer class. I approached him and said, "Hi, Mr. Campbell. Your son and I both have something in common--Lipscomb College!" It wasn't *exactly* true, but I was reaching for any way to start a conversation.

"Well, what do you know!" Archie said. "Phil is here in Knoxville, at our home. Why don't you come with me after the show and say hello?"

Again, I thought, *What do I have to lose? I'm on my way back to Abilene to work at the bank.* When the concert ended I followed Archie to his house. As we entered, he yelled, "Hey, Phil! One of your friends from college came home with me!" Phil Campbell walked in the room and looked at me, totally bewildered. He had never seen me before in his life.

I was really on the spot now. But I stepped up and gave it my best performance. "Hey, Phil!" I said with a smile. "Long time no see!" I can imagine him searching his mind to remember where we might have met. And I think he was embarrassed that he didn't recognize me. But he was gracious and friendly, and we had a nice time visiting. By the end of the night we had gotten to know each other pretty well, so I pulled out my guitar and Phil got out his banjo. We had fun playing music and even wrote a song together, which we called *Place Within My Mind*.

Archie seemed to take a liking to me, and before I left he mentioned that he was going to be working in Gatlinburg over the summer and he needed someone to house-sit at his home in Nashville. Would I be interested in doing that?

Of course, I would.

My "Hail Mary" had worked. I was going back to Nashville.

## Mister Guitar

I ended up spending the rest of that summer and the next at Archie Campbell's home in Brentwood, near Nashville. It was the beginning of a new season for me. Archie was a well-known and beloved figure in Nashville. When he came back to town he took me with him to meet other people in the music business. One morning he brought me to the Pancake Pantry, a popular restaurant where industry folks would come for a casual breakfast. Suddenly I found myself sitting shoulder-to-shoulder with the top executives in the business, including the legendary Chet Atkins.

Musicians know Chet Atkins as one of the best guitarists ever to pick up the instrument. In fact, one of his nicknames was *Mister Guitar*. As a musician and producer, Chet pretty much invented the "Nashville sound." And he helped build the country music industry into the powerhouse it became. Archie and Chet had been lifelong friends and I got to formally meet him when Archie took me over to his office at the RCA Victor office building. Archie told me he had asked Chet to be my mentor. Chet later told me he would make me a big star when the time was right. Even though that was not my goal, it was very encouraging at the time. I'm sure Chet's initial interest in me was in large part a result of Archie asking a favor of his long-time friend. By this time Chet was

CHET ATKINS          **RC/I** Records and Tapes
Exclusively On **RC/I**

the head of RCA's Nashville record division—and probably the most influential person in Nashville. Yet, I found him to be one of the most generous, humble and personable people I've ever met. He invited me to come visit with him in his office anytime.

And I did, over and over. We'd talk about music, songwriting, the business side, being a session musician, and just about everything else. Chet always gave his time freely and was a great help to me as I tried to find

my place in Music City. At that time thousands of aspiring musicians were coming to Nashville every year. And every one of them would have given anything to meet Chet Atkins. I feel supremely blessed that he took the time to befriend me. One weekend, Archie came back to town to perform at the Grand Ole Opry and invited me to come with him. It would be my first time visiting the famous Ryman Auditorium. When we got there Archie took me backstage. The singer Dottie West was also performing that evening. She had brought a young songwriter with her that she'd discovered. He and I struck up a conversation.

"Where are you from?" I asked him.

"Odessa, Texas."

"That's funny. I'm from Abilene, Texas. What's your name?"

"Larry Gatlin."

As I found out, Larry had also lived in Abilene growing up, so we had that in common too. Of course, he went on to a long, successful career as a songwriter and performer. Dottie West had hits with several of his

songs, as did Elvis Presley. Then Larry, and his brothers broke out as performers in their own right, scoring big hits on the pop and country charts. But that evening at the Ryman Auditorium we were just two struggling musicians hoping for a break, and that gave us a special bond. We remain friends to this day, but we have a little disagreement about that first meeting. Larry remembers convincing Mr. Bell—the security guard at the Ryman–to sneak me into the back of the auditorium. And I remember meeting him backstage. Either way, that was the first time we met, and the beginning of a great friendship.

Soon Larry's brothers, Steve and Rudy, moved to town. They needed somewhere to stay, so they lived with me at Archie's house for a few days until they could find a place of their own. That's how Nashville was in those days—a lot of people struggling to find their place in the music scene and helping each other along the way. When I finally moved into my own apartment, Larry gave me a couch he and his wife Janice had made when they got married. It was handmade with material that looked like pony hides. You could call it a one-of-a-kind, or just plain ugly. But I was so thrilled to have a couch. We still laugh about that sofa.

## Adventures with Jerry Reed

After my second summer in Nashville I decided to stay in town for the fall and take classes at Lipscomb College. But I knew that Opryland would be closing for the season, so I'd need another job. I was visiting with Chet Atkins in his office one day and mentioned my predicament to him. Right away he picked up the phone and called his good friend Jerry Reed. "I have my friend Chris Christian here," Chet told Jerry. "He's a good kid. Do you think you could find some work for him?"

That began my wild adventure with Jerry Reed. He was famous as a singer-songwriter, and as a first-rate fingerstyle guitar picker. Jerry specialized in humorous, hard-hitting, country-flavored story songs with titles like *Alabama Wild Man, You Took All the Ramblin' Out of Me*, and *She Got the Gold Mine (I Got the Shaft)*. His 1971 crossover hit, *When You're Hot, You're Hot*, sold a million copies and won him a Grammy.

It turned out, Jerry had an eight-track recording studio and needed someone to manage and clean it up. He knew I was an aspiring musician, so he offered me a deal: If I would take care of his office and studio during the day, I could use the recording studio at night—as long as I was ready to work the next morning. He also said he'd listen to some of my songs to see if there were any he might record himself.

I accepted immediately. And later, he did record two of my songs.

In my new job, I was at the studio during the day with Jerry and his manager Harry Warner. At night, I invited all my struggling musician friends over. We recorded our own songs and experimented with various techniques, often working till midnight. Then I spent the wee morning hours adding overdubs, mixing, and learning how everything worked. I needed more understanding of things like how to equalize (EQ) the bass, treble and midranges. Those long hours deepened my knowledge of engineering and taught me how to paint a musical canvas. That helped later, when I began playing most of the instruments on my recordings and knowing how to engineer became even more crucial.

If we were finished by eight a.m. sharp, this was all okay with Jerry. I didn't realize it at the time, but that learning experience helped me get past a dilemma that all aspiring producers face: No one wants to hire a producer without a track record, but you can't get a track record without producing. I had no prior experience as a producer, but I was learning the recording process with all those late-night sessions at Jerry's. I was just recording demos and jingles, but it was invaluable experience just the same. I soon got many opportunities to produce. And when they came, they hit like a tidal wave.

Jerry and Chet Atkins would sometimes hit the road on weekends and do concerts together. After I'd been working for Jerry a few months, they began inviting me to come along with them and play guitar. That was quite an honor—and a fun experience too. They often shared the

stage with other big stars, such as Willie Nelson. It was always exciting to meet the musicians I'd heard of and admired.

The group that played with Chet and Jerry was amazing in itself. Sometimes Jerry would put away his guitar and just sing. And then Paul Yandell would take over on guitar. During down times, Paul spent hours teaching me Jerry's guitar licks and unique fingerpicking style. His way of playing was counterintuitive, kind of like playing a five-string banjo. Those times with Paul are among my most cherished memories of learning the guitar. The keyboard player was a guy named Randy Goodrum, who went on to write the hits *Oh Sherrie* and *Foolish Heart* for Steve Perry, *You Needed Me* for Anne Murray, and *Bluer than Blue* for Michael Johnson. He is one of the great songwriters of our time. Another band member was Rodney Crowell, who went on to play with Emmylou Harris and later formed The Cherry Bombs—a group that included a great guitarist named Vince Gill. Vince had a great solo career and later married Amy Grant. Two other members of The Cherry Bombs were drummer Larrie Londin and pianist Tony Brown—both of whom played an important role in my career in Nashville. It is truly a small world!

On one of those out-of-town gigs, Chet and Jerry were invited to a Humana Challenge Golf Tournament along with several other big country acts. There was an award gala at the end of the tournament where all the celebrities performed. Before I knew it, I was backstage jamming with Chet Atkins, Jerry Reed, Roy Clark, Glen Campbell and John Hartford—each one a legendary musician in his own right. What an amazing experience for a fourth-grade ukulele player from Mrs. Patterson's class!

Jerry Reed was a one-of-a-kind character who had some funny quirks. One of them was that he was an obsessive fan of the Vanderbilt University football team. Whenever Vanderbilt was playing on the same night as one of his shows, Jerry would end the show early and rush back to the hotel. Then he called his wife, Priscilla, in Nashville and asked her to put the phone next to the radio. He'd lie in bed listening to the entire game on the phone. This was a time when long-distance calls were very expensive, so there's no telling what that habit cost him. But that was Jerry.

He was also notorious for his practical jokes. One year when Chet's birthday came around, Jerry decided to throw him a birthday party. He told Chet to invite all his friends to a little Italian restaurant on West End Boulevard near Vanderbilt University. Everyone came, and Jerry encouraged them all to order whatever they wanted. "Eat!" he told them. "Drink up! One more round for everyone! Deserts for everyone!" But when the bill came at the end, Jerry left the table, got in his car and went home. So, Chet Atkins got to pay for his own birthday party.

Actually, Chet probably laughed more than anyone else. Jerry was generous to a fault, helping Chet out all the time in many ways—including giving me a job!

Jerry was friends with Elvis Presley, and I was always fascinated when Jerry would tell Elvis stories. Elvis had recorded several of Jerry's songs, including *A Thing Called Love*, and *Talk about the Good Times*. On one occasion, Elvis was driving down Ventura Boulevard in L.A. and heard Jerry's song *Guitar Man* on the radio. Elvis decided to record his own version of Jerry's song, *Guitar Man*. But during the session, the guitarist couldn't quite duplicate Jerry's unique guitar style. Elvis told Felton Jarvis, the producer, "Get Jerry in here! He needs to play the guitar part!" So, Felton called Jerry and found out he was fishing on the Cumberland River.

Felton convinced Jerry to come play guitar on his song and in a short time Jerry showed up at the recording studio. Here's how Felton remembers it:

> When he arrived, he looked like a sure-enough Alabama wild man. You know, he hadn't shaved in about a week, and he had them old clogs on—that was just the way he dressed. He come in, and Elvis looked at him and said, "Lord, have mercy, what is that?"

Jerry told me he had indeed been fishing and probably smelled like a carp and he saw no reason to change his clothes. After all, there was no dress code at Elvis sessions. He said, "I wouldn't have changed if there was one". Jerry pulled out his electric gut-string guitar, gave it a special tuning and they launched into *Guitar Man* again.

Here's Jerry's recollection of what followed:

> He said, "As soon as the band hit the intro, you could see Elvis' eyes light up and he knew they had it. Elvis cut the song a lot faster than I did and it turned into a ho-down. I guess because he got excited. By the third or fourth take I got pumped, and then Elvis got pumped, and the more he got pumped up, the more I did. It was like a snowball effect."

> By the next take, Elvis was finally happy. And that was the record.

## A Fateful Phone Call

One day the phone rang at Archie's home and I picked it up. "Is Phil Campbell there?" the caller asked.

"No, he's not."

"Well, this is John Haywood. I'm the entertainment director at Opryland, and we need a banjo player. We want to know if Phil might want to play banjo for us." Opryland was a new Nashville theme park that was set to open the following spring. It was going to be very music-oriented, so they needed to hire lots of musicians.

"Well, Phil's not in town, but I'm a banjo player."

Oh, really?"

"Yeah, Phil's working with his dad up in Gatlinburg. When can I see you?"

"Well, could you come in tomorrow morning? We've got a short time frame here."

"Sure," I said. The next day I drove in and auditioned. And just like that, I was hired as the first banjo player in the Dixieland band at Opryland. Over the next couple of years, that job provided me with a nice reliable income. But it was also much more. At Opryland, three great things happened that would change the course of my life. But I'll get to that later.

## Monument Studios

Gary S. Paxton was a well-known musician and producer in Nashville. He had a reputation for being, let's say, *colorful*. One of his albums was titled *The Astonishing, Outrageous, Amazing, Incredible, Unbelievable, Different World of Gary S. Paxton*. That described it pretty well. Gary had made a splash in 1959 as part of the duo Skip and Flip. Their song *It Was I* sold a million copies, followed by *Cherry Pie*, which was also a big hit. He had another big seller with the novelty song *Alley Oop*, which he recorded under the name the Hollywood Argyles. And he produced yet another novelty song, *Monster Mash* by Bobby "Boris" Pickett, which became, well, a monster hit.

After that, Gary had some ups and downs, but by the time I met him in Nashville he had become a Christian and was working at Monument Studios, owned by Fred Foster—the same man who had given my songs a listen when I first came to town. Coincidentally, Fred was the one who signed Larry Gatlin and his brothers to his label Monument Records, paving their way to stardom.

Gary Paxton heard that I had played with Chet Atkins and Jerry Reed. So one day he called me. "We need another guitar player in our group that records at Monument," he said. "It's only fifty dollars a day, but at least you'll have some work." I said okay.

Aspiring artists would come to Monument Studios to make custom records, which they would market on their own rather than through a label. Some of them were country acts hoping to make it big in Music City, USA. Others were gospel quartets that traveled the country singing at churches and revival meetings. They stopped in at the studio just long enough to create an album they could take on the road to sell. And at Monument Studios, they could do that fast. They might start a recording session at eight in the morning, and by nine that evening they'd walk out with an acetate of their album. I'm pretty sure most of those records weren't very good, but they were definitely fast and cheap.

Needless to say, it was kind of an assembly-line process. The songs usually weren't complicated, so we musicians could learn them quickly. A lot of us were self-taught anyway and didn't read music. The chord charts we used had numbers—1, 4, 5, etc.—instead of letter designations like C, F or G. That way, if a key didn't suit a particular singer, we could change keys in a flash instead of rewriting all the charts. The gospel quartets all tended to have similar repertoires, so after recording the same songs countless times we often didn't need charts.

Monument employed a lot of musicians who went on to have great careers. Tony Brown was one of the piano players on many of those quartet sessions, and he and I became good friends. He had played with the Oak Ridge Boys before they became a popular crossover act; and the Stamps Quartet, who opened for Elvis Presley. He also backed Emmylou Harris and Roseanne Cash. Tony played with Elvis on his last tour and on his last album, *Moody Blue*, which was recorded in the Jungle Room at Graceland. With the help of his mentor Jimmy Bowen, Tony became one of the greatest producers Nashville has ever seen, producing artists such as Reba McIntyre, Wynonna Judd, Rodney Crowell, Steve Earl, Patty Loveless, George Strait and Vince Gill. He eventually produced more than 100 number-one country hits (that's right, *more than a hundred!*).

At Monument I also became very good friends with a singer named Sean Nielsen (who later changed his first name to Sherrill). Besides his studio work, he became a backup singer for Elvis Presley. He and I would often share songs with each other. One night as we were jamming I sang *Love Song of the Year* for him, a song I wrote as a junior in high school. Sherrill liked it enough to learn it. And soon he was singing it for another friend of his—Elvis.

Ch 4. Off to Music City with $100

# 5

# The Best Things Happen at Opryland

The Ryman Auditorium in downtown Nashville had been the home of the Grand Ole Opry since 1943. But by the '70s it was falling into disrepair—just as country music was growing more popular than ever. So, the company that owned the Opry decided to find a bigger venue that could serve as an all-around entertainment destination. They bought a large piece of land next to the Cumberland River and built the new Opry building along with a huge array of other attractions. They called it Opryland USA. It was a full-on amusement park, but the real focus was music—and not just country music, either. There were nine sections, each one devoted to a particular style of American music. The rides had names like "the Rock 'n Roller Coaster" and "the Dulcimer Splash."

Beginning my second summer in Nashville, I was the banjo player in Opryland's Dixieland band. We had a drummer, a tuba player, a trumpet player and a trombone player, and we all wore pink bowties and straw hats. We strolled down the lane in the New Orleans area playing *When the Saints Go Marching In*. Then we stepped

into a white gazebo and played more Dixieland songs for about fifteen minutes, then we strolled back to our trailer, playing as we went. We did this five times a day. Needless to say, this was not what I'd pictured myself doing when I was driving to Nashville that first time. But it was a job. I was playing music. And I was paying the bills.

## Meeting Shanon

Opryland had young employees who walked around with little dust-bins picking up trash. And one of them in the New Orleans section really caught my eye. She had thin legs and dark hair down to her waist. She was wearing a little apron. And boy, was she cute. One day as she passed by, I said, "Hey, is that Shalimar you're wearing?"

It was a bold line, but hey, I was the banjo player at Opryland, which made me pretty cool. And it just so happened that one of my girl-friends in high school had worn Shalimar perfume, so I recognized the scent right away.

She gave me a sly look. "Yeah. How'd you know?"

That's how it started. As we began to talk I found out that her name was Shanon. She was from a good family in Nashville and didn't really need to work. She was enrolled at Vanderbilt University for the fall, but her father had told her, "Shanon, you need to get a job for the summer before you go to college." She thought, *I want to earn spending money. But I'd like to get a tan.* By working at Opryland, she could get paid to get a tan! So here she was, sweeping trash in the New Orleans section.

As Shanon told me later, she thought I was full of myself. The girls at Opryland would talk among themselves, and she said, "The word was out on you!" I was known for dating girls once and then dropping them. That might seem callous now, but I felt I was just being realistic. I wanted a long-term relationship. If I saw that the right ingredients weren't there, why prolong things?

But with Shanon it was different. I knew within a day or two that I wanted to marry her. I began to seriously pursue her, and at one point I gave her a Bible. That opened up an opportunity to begin talking about the Scriptures and things of God. Shanon had been raised in the Methodist church but wasn't too serious about her faith then. As time went on that would change in a big way. Now, she's the finest example I know of a godly woman—right up there with my grandmother. I'm glad that they got to know each other before Monkey passed away on November 18, 1975.

But in the summer of 1973 Shanon and I were just starting to date. I drove up to her parents' house in my long, bodacious silver Cadillac and honked for her to come outside. I wasn't trying to be rude. I was just afraid to face her parents.

I could imagine their conversations:

"So, who's this guy you're dating?"

"Well, he's a musician. He plays the guitar at Shakey's Pizza. And he also plays the banjo at Opryland—in a straw hat and pink bowtie!"

Not a promising picture.

Now that I'm a dad myself, I sometimes tease Shanon's father: "How could you have even let me get near your daughter back then?" But he did. And it eventually worked out well.

After two summers in Nashville, I knew this was where I belonged. But I also wanted to complete my college degree. So I went back to Abilene Christian College and made it through my senior year. When I finished my last exam, I walked straight out to the parking lot, got in my car—which was already packed—and hit the highway. No graduation ceremony. No waiting around for a diploma (which they sent later). I was headed for Nashville—where my future was waiting. I didn't think my business degree would help much in the music world. But I found out that in the *music business*, that second word is just as important as the first.

My speakers and musical instruments were piled in the back of my black Chevy station wagon and my clothes were in a chest of drawers strapped to the top. As I drove east on Highway 20 I was thinking about the exciting things that might await me. Then, just a few miles out of town, I heard a sudden crashing noise. As I looked in my rearview mirror I saw my chest of drawers bouncing off the pavement and my underwear scattering in the wind. I pulled off to the shoulder and spent the next few hair-raising minutes scrambling in and out of traffic retrieving what was left of my belongings.

Not a great start. But I was still optimistic.

Soon I was back in Nashville, playing the banjo at Opryland in my straw hat and pink bowtie. So far, two wonderful things had happened to me there: I'd got to play music in a professional setting, and I met the love of my life. Now I was about to experience a third life-changing event.

## Meeting Wayne Newton

A production team came to Opryland to film a TV special featuring Tennessee Ernie Ford, Carol Lawrence, Petula Clark and Wayne Newton. Wayne had built a long career as a pop star with hits such as *Danke Schoen, Daddy, Don't You Walk So Fast*, and *Red Roses for a Blue Lady*. The production team wanted to film a musical number with Wayne on the riverboat as it floated down the Cumberland River next to Opryland. And they needed a banjo player for the shoot. The music tracks had already been recorded in a Los Angeles studio, but the banjo player would pretend to accompany Wayne as he lip-synced the vocal. Since I was the banjo player in the Dixieland band, they asked me to be in the shoot. I was pleased, but also alarmed. "I don't know that song Wayne's going to be singing!" I told them.

"That's okay," they told me. "You just need to look like you're playing." I quickly got the idea and made my TV debut pretending to play alongside Wayne Newton. The shoot took all day, and between takes Wayne and I had lots of time to talk and get to know each other. Toward the end, he turned to me and said, "When Opryland closes, why don't you come to Las Vegas and play in my band?"

Las Vegas? I was a Church of Christ boy from Abilene. He might as well have asked me to go to Mars. I didn't give his invitation much thought. Besides, Wayne hadn't yet heard me play a note! He knew I was a musician, but how could he know I was good enough to play in his band?

That brings to mind something important that I've learned over the years. Young musicians often ask me for advice on how to "make it" in the business. I tell them, "Be nice." If people like you, they'll want to have you around. If you're a jerk, they won't. When Chet Atkins referred me to Jerry Reed, he didn't say *here's Chris, he's a great guitar player*, or, *he's a great songwriter*. He said, "Here's Chris. He's a great kid." Simply being agreeable is what got me in the door. People often say it's *who you know* that matters. I would say it's not who you know—but who likes you. Talent matters, of course. But being an agreeable and friendly person is just as important.

A few days after the taping with Wayne Newton on the river boat, toward the end of the Opryland season, the phone rang at our Dixieland band trailer. Bob Phillips, one of our horn players, picked it up. "Chris, it's for you," he said. "He says he's calling for Wayne Newton."

I took the phone and heard Mitch Greenberg, Wayne's assistant, say, "Wayne would like for you to come to Vegas this weekend. There's a ticket waiting for you at the airport."

# 6

# Mister Las Vegas

When I arrived in Las Vegas at the end of the summer in 1973, I had no idea what to expect. But it was clearly going to be an adventure. Up till then my most exciting journey had been driving to Nashville from Abilene. Now here I was in the glitz capital of the world—at the invitation of Mr. Las Vegas himself. In those days Wayne Newton was the highest-paid entertainer in town. He was the headliner at the Sands Hotel. And he arranged to put me up in a penthouse suite there.

On the first night, Wayne invited me to watch his show. Then I went backstage afterward to greet him. Wayne and his band always met together for about twenty minutes after each show to discuss what went right, what went wrong, and anything else anyone wanted to talk about. When I joined them, Wayne came up to me and cordially asked, "What'd you think of the show?"

"Oh, it was great!" I said. And I wasn't kidding. Wayne Newton was and is a consummate entertainer. With his five-piece band and a fifty-person orchestra too, Wayne put on a show like I had never seen.

"Well, good. Come back tomorrow night at seven."

The show started each night at eight o'clock, and Wayne gathered with his band at seven. I did as he suggested. When I went backstage that second night, he said, "Did you enjoy the Sands and seeing Las Vegas? I've got the same spot reserved for you, so why don't you go watch the show again? Every night's a little different."

So, I watched the show again—and went backstage again afterward. Wayne and the band were in a great mood, laughing and cutting up. At the end, Wayne said "Have some fun tomorrow and I'll see you back here tomorrow night at seven."

I was beginning to think Wayne had changed his mind about having me in his band. After all, he hadn't mentioned a thing about it since I arrived. And I was scheduled to fly back to Nashville the following day. I watched the show again and went backstage again afterward. I met Wayne in his dressing room. "Mr. Newton," I began, "I really appreciate the opportunity to come out and see your show. I'd never been to Las Vegas before. It's been really exciting. But my flight is tomorrow morning. I'm going to be heading back to Nashville."

Wayne just looked at me. Then, to my amazement, he said, "When can you start?"

After a few seconds I regained my composure and said I'd just need to go back to Nashville, get my clothes and instruments, and drive back.

I could start in one week. As I was leaving the meeting, Mitch Greenberg followed me out. "You'll make $500 a week," he told me. "You'll have a penthouse on top of the Sands and you can charge anything you want to Wayne's account." The next morning, I packed my guitar, banjo and suitcase—all I had brought—and flew home. Then I loaded up my car and drove straight back to Las Vegas.

One week after my last day at Opryland, I was playing guitar for Wayne Newton at the Sands Hotel. One of the band members took the time to teach me the songs in the show, and by the third day I was ready to go. We played from eight to ten o'clock each night. Wayne opened the show with a fifteen-minute teaser. After that, Dave Barry, a veteran Borscht-belt comedian, did a twenty-five-minute comedy routine. Then Wayne would come out and give a great performance every single night for an hour and a half. As part of his five-piece rhythm section I played guitar, five-string banjo and harmonica, often performing duets with Wayne. In addition to his rhythm section, Wayne was accompanied by the Don Vincent Orchestra and the Jive Sisters singing background vocals.

Playing for Wayne Newton gave me a unique opportunity to work up close with one of the world's great entertainers, night after night. For Wayne, performing in front of an audience was like oxygen. He thrived on it. Their enthusiasm would push him to do what seemed like a better show every night. One of his great talents was to make everyone in the audience feel they had come on the best night of the year—even though the set remained basically the same.

I discovered that, along with music, Wayne's other great love was Polish Arabian horses. He kept up to eighty-five horses at his ranch outside Las Vegas, which he named *Casa de Shenandoah*. Over the next few months, when we had days off I sometimes spent time with him there. Learning about Arabian horses from Wayne proved helpful later when I worked for Word Records in Waco, Texas. It turned out that Jerrell McCracken, Word's founder and president, had the largest Egyptian Arabian horse collection in the United States. But there was a difference: Wayne believed Polish Arabians were the top breed, and Jerrell was convinced that Egyptian Arabians were. Who was right? I have no idea. But both were very passionate about their horses.

After a while my life in Las Vegas began to take on a routine quality. I didn't smoke, drink, gamble or chase women, so the things that attracted most people to the city didn't hold much appeal for me. I awakened and went to Denny's for breakfast. I spent some time reading the Bible, and maybe worked on the lyrics to some song I was writing. Then I went to the swimming pool for about an hour to get a tan. Then it was back to the penthouse until show time. About a month into my stay, I got an idea. Why not use all those daylight hours to learn the instruments I didn't yet know how to play? So, I went to a local music store and bought every instrument I could think of that I hadn't learned yet—a fiddle, an autoharp, harmonicas in every key, a drum pad with sticks, and even a steel guitar. I had instruments lying all over the penthouse. It looked like a music store! I imagine the maids must have had a few laughs when they came in to clean up. Anyway, I began spending about six hours a day learning how to play each instrument and getting better on the ones I already knew.

In his shows, Wayne would play *Orange Blossom Special* on the fiddle. So I asked him to teach it to me, which he kindly did. But as I discovered, the violin is one of the hardest instruments to learn. And when a person is just starting, it really sounds awful! I spent hours on the penthouse balcony practicing *Orange Blossom Special* on my new fiddle. One night at the after-show band meeting, one of the guys said, "Hey, did you all hear about that crazy guy screeching away on the violin on his balcony?" None of them knew it was me. And I kept my mouth shut.

I didn't become a virtuoso on any of those instruments, but I learned a few songs on each one. Most importantly, I discovered what each instrument was capable of. This became extremely important later when

I was a producer working with the best musicians in Nashville. What I'd learned enabled me to communicate and explain exactly what I wanted from each instrument.

## Mr. Hughes

Howard Hughes owned nine hotel-casinos in Las Vegas, including the Sands, the Desert Inn, and the Frontier. In fact, 15 percent of the gambling revenue in Vegas went through a Hughes-owned hotel. This was ironic, since Hughes himself did not smoke, drink or gamble. That was probably the only thing he and I had in common, other than both being from Texas.

Back then, the marquee at the Sands Hotel said, "Walter Kane presents Wayne Newton." Walter was the entertainment director for all of Howard Hughes' Vegas hotels, as well as his close friend and associate. Since Wayne Newton was the top act in all of those properties, Walter would come to his shows. And I often had the opportunity to visit with him afterwards. I was never shy about meeting people or asking questions, so one day I asked Walter if there was any chance I might meet his boss, Mr. Hughes.

He said, "I'll see what I can do."

A few weeks later Walter came to the Sands again. And he asked me to come over to the Desert Inn—another Hughes hotel—after Wayne's show. I was intrigued. The headliner at the Desert Inn at that time was the singer Bobbie Gentry, who had scored a big hit in 1967 with her song, *Ode to Billy Joe*. When I went to see Walter there I found myself backstage in Bobbie's green room. Walter left us there to talk for about half an hour, so I got to know her a little bit. Then he came back and said "Chris, let's go!" Walter and I took the elevator to the ninth floor, which served as Howard Hughes' living quarters. (His business offices occupied the eighth floor.) When we got out, Walter walked me down the hall and opened a door. There, just beyond the door, was a screen. I never saw the person behind it, but Walter introduced him to me as Mr. Hughes.

I said something like, "Hello, Mr. Hughes, I'm very glad to meet you. I've loved working at your Sands Hotel with Wayne Newton and I appreciate the opportunity you and Wayne have given me."

He said, "I'm pleased to meet you. I understand you're doing a good job. We're glad to have you working for us." There were a few more words exchanged and then we left. So I had met Howard Hughes. But I never *saw* him! To put things in perspective, Hughes was not yet the mysterious, legendary figure he would become. He was just a very wealthy, famous, and eccentric man who happened to own the hotel I worked at. So I guess I considered him my ultimate boss. I was glad to meet him. But it was certainly one of the strangest experiences of my time in Las Vegas.

## Recording My Own Music

I was practicing my instruments in the penthouse all day, playing a two-hour show at night, and then doing it all over again the next day. Sometimes we went to Harrah's in Lake Tahoe for a few nights, but we were still doing the same show. After about four months of that I began to go stir-crazy. Playing the same songs over and over wasn't what I envisioned when I saw Dow Patterson play his song in Mrs. Patterson's class. I wasn't like Wayne, who lived to perform and entertain audiences. As long as he was pleasing the audience and receiving applause, he was in his element. But I just wanted to create. And I couldn't do that performing the same songs night after night.

One day Wayne asked me, "Are you enjoying this?" I appreciated his interest and concern, but I felt I needed to be honest.

"Yeah," I said, "I'm really enjoying it. But I miss creating. I've got all these songs I've been writing, and I'd really like to go into a studio and get them demoed."

The next day, Wayne pulled me aside and said, "I called Paul Anka. He's got a studio here in town and I booked some time there for you. So, during the day, why don't you go over there and record your demos? I'll pay for it." That was Wayne—always considerate, always generous. He also added "And let me hear them when you're done!"

For the next week or two, I spent the days recording my songs at Paul Anka's Vegas studio. Wayne's other band members were also kind enough to come and help. Recording made the days go by much faster. And I came out of it with new demos of my songs. Among them were *Sunshine Lady*, *Fighting the Forgotten Feeling*, and *Ballad of Ollie Hand*, which ended up being used in a feature film, *The No Mercy Man*.

But what really emerged from all that was a realization: *This* was what I wanted and needed to be doing—all day every day. My path was crystal-clear. I needed to *create*. I kept working with Wayne for another month. But that restless feeling in my gut was only growing stronger. And then something happened at the Hilton International in late January 1974 that radically changed my direction. It was time for a conversation that I wasn't looking forward to.

# 7

# Elvis and Me

"You're not going to believe this!"

It was Sherrill Nielsen on the phone, my friend from Monument Studios. He was calling from Memphis, all excited about what had happened at Graceland just the night before. He'd spent the evening there with Elvis and his friends singing gospel songs, as they often did. After a few hours, Elvis said, "Somebody sing me some new songs." That's when Sherrill told him he had a friend who'd written a song he really liked.

"Sing it to me," Elvis said.

Sherrill broke into *Love Song of the Year* and by the time he finished, Elvis was tearing up. "That reminds me of Priscilla," he said. "I've got to record that song!"

That was early 1973—before I ever met Wayne Newton or moved to Las Vegas. But it was a great encouragement to me as a songwriter to have that affirmation from a real music legend. As a songwriter, you often hear things that sound exciting at the time, but don't end up happening. I was hopeful and called my parents with the news, and wrote Monkey to pray, but then I just tucked it away.

I have always marveled at the many amazing people God has brought into my life. Often, those relationships are woven into a tapestry that later leads to a life-changing event that only God could orchestrate. Meeting Sherill Nielsen was certainly one of those instances.

A little more about Sherill: One of the great gospel tenors of his day, he had sung with the Imperials, the Blackwood Brothers, and several other popular quartets. Elvis loved gospel music all his life, so Sherrill's voice caught his ear too. He has even been quoted saying that Sherrill Nielsen was his favorite singer.

As most Elvis fans know, he regularly used gospel quartets as his back-up singers. One of those groups was the Stamps Quartet, led by the legendary bass singer J.D. Sumner, with his nephew Donnie Sumner singing lead. But in 1972, Donnie left the group. This distressed Elvis. He had always liked Donnie and felt bad for his friend. So he gave Donnie a friendly suggestion. Why don't we form a new  group? That sounded like a good idea, so Elvis recruited singer Tim Beatty, and Sherrill Nielsen, to create VOICE, INC. Elvis had Charlie Hodge bring Donnie, Tim, and Sherrill to meet him. Elvis drew up an impromptu contract written in ballpoint pen on a sheet of bathroom tissue which read: "I, Elvis Aaron Presley, agree to pay to Donnie Sumner, Sean [Sherrill] Nielsen, and Tim Beatty over the next 12 months the sum total of $100,000 dollars for their full time service to sing at my request." Elvis named the group. They began backing up Elvis *along with* the Stamps Quartet.

Elvis didn't need three more singers in his touring group. And I would guess his manager, Colonel Parker, was not happy about paying for them. But Elvis wanted them, so they became part of his show. He liked Sherrill and Donnie and was always happy to have friends around him. Of course, he also knew they wouldn't mind having a good, steady pay-check. This was just one of many examples of Elvis' legendary generosity. As the people close to him found out, money was not important to Elvis. Friends were. Sam Thompson, who worked as his bodyguard, put it this way: "I didn't know Elvis to ever think about money, or even have money. He relied on his entourage and bodyguards to take care of his small personal expenses here and there, and Elvis always took care of them."

That freedom with money sometimes irked Colonel Parker, who was always trying to protect and look out for Elvis. When members of the crew would come back to the Colonel for reimbursements, he asked them, "Did you get a receipt?" The answer, of course, was no. (Can you imagine loaning $100 to Elvis Presley—and asking him for a receipt?) So, to avoid that problem some of the guys started wearing pants without pockets. That way, when Elvis asked them for cash they could say, "Sorry, E. I don't have my wallet!"

Elvis' association with Sherrill and VOICE, Inc. would last until Elvis's death in 1977.

## Meeting the King of Rock and Roll

Meanwhile, Elvis did indeed record *Love Song of the Year*, on December 12, 1973 at Stax Studio in Memphis. It was the first song I had written that someone else recorded—and that someone just happened to be Elvis Presley. That was like winning the jackpot on the first try! To make it even more unlikely, this was a song I wrote as a junior in high school.

Elvis' recording would not be released for more than a year, but people in the music business tend to find out about these things. So, just having a song recorded by the king of rock and roll quickly raised my visibility in Nashville.

But when all this happened, I was in the middle of my ongoing job with Wayne Newton in Las Vegas. One day in January 1974, I received a call from Red West, a member of Elvis' "Memphis Mafia." "Elvis would like to invite you to his opening night at the Las Vegas Hilton," Red said, "and to come up to his suite after the midnight show."

How could I say no? I had never met Elvis before and was excited at the thought. But I had a little problem. Wayne Newton dominated Las Vegas in those days, but there was just one entertainer who could compete with him—Elvis Presley. I was about to ask my boss for a night off from his show—so I could go meet his only competition in Vegas. I wasn't relishing the prospect. When I finally approached Wayne and asked for a night off, he kindly granted my request, and then asked me, "So, what are you going to do with your night off?" I had to tell him. I think it hit him like a punch in the gut, but he just smiled and said, "Of course you can. I'm so proud of you! That sounds like a great opportunity. Tell Elvis hello for me." That was Wayne—always gracious.

The next night, I went to the Las Vegas Hilton with a friend from Nashville named Steve. We walked into the lobby where Red West met us. He directed us to a special horseshoe-shaped booth they had reserved for us in the front of the showroom. It was a perfect spot for watching the show, and Elvis gave two fantastic performances. After the midnight show, we were ushered backstage and then up to the penthouse suite.

This was Elvis Presley's after-show party for his opening night at the Las Vegas Hilton. There was not a bigger ticket in the world. And I was a twenty-two-year-old kid from Abilene, soaking it all in. There were so many celebrities, dignitaries and VIP's present that I couldn't count them all. I figured I might just sit in the corner and watch, and then go home. But after a while, Elvis walked over to me and said, "Hello Chris, my name is Elvis Presley."

*As if I didn't know who he was.* I had just attended *his* show, at *his* invitation, and now here I was at *his* after-show party. But with his humble southern manners, Elvis Presley, the king of rock and roll, felt obliged to introduce himself. I found out later this was normal for him. I tried hard to keep my composure. But meanwhile, my friend Steve was hyperventilating. "I can't believe it!" he said, almost shouting. "Elvis Presley! I can't believe it! Elvis Presley!" I was mortified and gave Elvis an apologetic look out of the corner of my eye. He just winked as if to say *don't worry about it.* I'm sure he got that kind of reaction a lot.

As we talked, Elvis mentioned how much he loved my song and in fact, he wanted everyone in the room to hear it. Then he stood up, clapped his hands, and asked for everyone to be quiet. As a hush fell over the room, Elvis said, "This is Chris Christian. A few months ago I heard a song he wrote, and it touched me. I recorded it recently and he's never heard my version of the song. I thought it would be fun for Chris and all of you to hear it for the first time. I hope you like it."

Needless to say, I felt a little embarrassed and deeply honored. He cued up the record and as it began he put his arm around me. And then I was hearing Elvis Presley singing my song for the very first time. What a surprise, honor, and thrill. The record was an acetate—a one-off disc that serves as a master for the vinyl records that follow. That's how new this recording was.

As the song ended and everyone clapped, Elvis looked at me and whispered in my ear, "So how do you like what I did with your song?"

Elvis was the number-one rock star in the world—there was no number two. And he routinely recorded songs from the best songwriters in the world. But that night he was thoughtful enough to not just play my song for everyone—but then to ask me what I thought of it. Songwriters don't usually get that kind of attention from any artist, let alone a top entertainer like Elvis. In fact, of the hundreds of songs I've written that were recorded by other artists since then, Elvis was the only one who ever asked what I thought of his version! He clearly knew what a big moment this was for me and wanted to make it as memorable as possible. And what he couldn't have known was that this was the first song I'd ever had recorded by a major artist.

To this day, that night remains one of the most memorable of my life. And it was typical of the Elvis I would come to know—always considerate of other people's feelings. *"Love Song of the Year"* was finally released in 1975 on the Elvis' album *Promised Land*, which went Gold and reached number one on the Billboard Country charts.

After that night I began spending more time around Elvis. He couldn't appear in public without causing a scene, but he was still a normal guy who loved to have fun.

As Tony Brown said, "He was just like any other guy, except he was Elvis."

Elvis often invited his friends, wherever they were, to come join him. From time to time I would get one of those invitations. He invited me to Memphis or to recording sessions in Los Angeles. These adventures would typically begin no earlier than midnight and go into the morning. Elvis would make special arrangements to have certain stores open at the mall, or he would reserve the Memphian Theater exclusively for his group. Being Elvis, he often had access to films weeks before their release.

One night I received a call from Lamar Fike, one of his gang. "Go to the airport," he said. "Elvis wants to take some of his buddies and go see a movie." Off I flew to Memphis, where I joined a group of about twenty others who had gathered at the Memphian Theater. Elvis had reserved it, so we all went in and sat down. But where was Elvis? That question was answered soon enough. Suddenly, out of nowhere, he jumped up from the front row and started throwing pizzas at everyone in their seats, laughing his head off. Then the lights dimmed, and we all settled in to watch a special showing of *Jonathan Livingston Seagull*—two weeks before its general release. It was just another day in the extraordinary life of Elvis Presley.

Ricky Stanley was Elvis' half-brother. While talking to him one day, I asked, "Why did Elvis call me (a nobody) to come down so often?"

He said, "One of the reasons that you had access to Elvis, was not only because of your music, but because you were a believer. Elvis didn't want to talk about roles in a movie. He wanted to talk about God."

Once while staying in Memphis for meetings at St. Jude, I had the opportunity to visit Stax Studios, where Elvis had recorded *Promised Land*, including *"Love Song of the Year."* I walked through the recording booths and the control room. And I remembered sitting in Abilene, writing that song as a junior in high school. I could never have imagined then that Elvis Presley would record it—and how that would change my life. And this was where it had all happened. It was a remarkable, somewhat eerie feeling and it made me grateful all over again.

During that same trip, I had the opportunity to visit Sun Studios for the first time where Elvis recorded in the early days. I was also invited to be George Klein's guest on the Sirius/XM Elvis channel. It was the first time I had been back to Memphis and it brought back many special memories of a magical time.

Years later, I was in Palm Springs, California, when I got a call from Greg McDonald who had worked for Colonel Parker. Both of them had lived in Palm Springs, as did Elvis from time to time. Greg mentioned that Elvis' old Palm Springs estate was about to change hands. Elvis had sold the house years before, and Greg himself had owned it for a while. But the current owner was moving out, so it seemed like a good opportunity to go see the house one last time. Greg and I hopped into the car and drove to Little Tuscany Estates, a neighborhood on the western edge of Palm Springs beneath the towering San Jacinto Mountains.

Elvis Palm Springs home

There it was, just as Greg remembered it—a long, low-slung Spanish-style home sheltered behind a white stone wall and wrought-iron fence. There we met Reno Fontana, the current owner who was in the process of moving out. He welcomed us in amidst the commotion. As we walked through the rooms and the pool area, Greg's memories came flooding back. He began to reminisce about the many magical times he'd spent there with Elvis so many years before. And he did have some great stories. But then we were jolted back to the present. The house didn't belong to Elvis anymore. The king of rock and roll was long gone. But for both of us, walking through that home brought back a lot of fun memories from years past.

Before we left the estate, I spotted an old RCA Victrola record player among the personal items in the living room, left over from the Elvis era. Reno Fontana noticed my interest. Greg casually mentioned to him that I collect mementos featuring Nipper, the RCA dog. To me, that image of a dog peering quizzically into a loudspeaker symbolizes the first recordings of the human voice. I've always treasured things that represent that moment in history. I actually have a very large Nipper collection at my office. That famous image is usually accompanied by the caption, "His Master's Voice."

A little-known fact is where the slogan *His Master's Voice* came from. Nipper is sitting on his master's casket. The sound from the Victrola is so realistic that  he thinks it's really *his master's voice*. If it weren't for the invention of man's recorded voice, there would not be a record business and I would be a banker.

Reno turned to me and asked, "Do you want the Victrola?" Of course, I said yes. I left with another Nipper souvenir for my collection—and a little piece of Elvis history.

# 8

# Nashville, Take Two

Wayne Newton must have sensed that something was up. It was February of 1974, and I had just spent six amazing months playing in his band. Working with Mr. Las Vegas, one of the world's great entertainers, was a once-in-a-lifetime experience. But it also confirmed something to me. I didn't want to spend my life playing the same songs over and over. I needed to *create*. Specifically, I needed to go back to Nashville and see if I could compete with all the talented songwriters and producers there. Eventually I approached Wayne after one of our post-show meetings. "Wayne, I appreciate all you've done for me," I began. "Working with you has been a wonderful opportunity. But since being here I've discovered something. I was meant to create music, not just play the same show every night. I need to go back to Nashville and see what I can accomplish in the recording industry."

Wayne understood and assured me, "If you ever decide to come back, your job will be waiting for you!" He knew how tough the record business was and I think he really believed I would be back. But somehow, I knew I wouldn't.

So I said goodbye and began the long drive back to Nashville, the city I'd left six months earlier. I had no assurance of a job—or anything else. In a way, it was like my first summer in

Nashville all over again. But this time, I had some serious professional experience under my belt. And after producing demos at Paul Anka's Las Vegas studio, I knew what it felt like to record my own songs. I definitely wanted more of that. I also at least had one song recorded by Elvis and I was excited about improving my songwriting skills and hopefully getting more songs recorded by other artists.

## Home Sweet Home Jingle Company

But I also had to find a way to earn money in the meantime. I began writing and producing advertising jingles. I started my own company, *Home Sweet Home Jingle Company*, which was my first effort to unite my music and business skills.

Soon I was writing jingles for Coca Cola, Stouffers, and a small fast food chain called Chick-fil-A. It may have been the first jingle they ever used. Because of that I got to know the remarkable Cathy Family that started Chick-fil-A. Thinking I might have had a small part in the early days of that company has always had a special place in my heart. I still admire and keep up with Dan Cathy today.

## More Adventures at Opryland

That summer of 1974, I was back at Opryland as the leader of the folk show band. Part of my job was to hire the rest of the group. I knew I could sing and play guitar, so that was covered. We found a bass player, and a talented woman named Karen McKay who played dulcimer. George Grove, our five-string banjo player, would go on to play with the Kingston Trio—a job he held for more than forty years. It was a good group, but we still needed someone to play fiddle and fill in on some other instruments. This was a perfect opportunity to bring in my

old college roommate, Brown Bannister. So I called him. "Hey, Brown, I've got a job for you at Opryland."

"Great. What will I be doing?"

"You're playing with me in the folk show."

'That's great. *What am I doing?'*

"Well, I have guitar, bass, mandolin, and banjo covered, but I need a fiddle player."

"Chris, you're crazy. I don't know how to play fiddle!"

"Well, you're still the fiddle player in the folk show. I told them you're a fast learner."

Brown went out and bought a fiddle and did his best to learn how to play it during the few weeks he had to practice. And then there we were, performing on stage at Opryland. Brown's limited skills didn't pose a problem—until we got to the John Denver song, *Thank God I'm a Country Boy*, which called for a fiddle solo. Here's how Brown remembers what happened then:

"Every time we came to that part, I'd step back from the mic about twelve feet and would just go to town. I'd smile like the fiddlers' smile, but nobody could ever hear me. They always clapped, though."

Just to be doubly sure Brown was protected, I always had the sound engineer turn his mic down during his solo.

By the end of the season we were all braindead from doing the same show five times a day, six days a week. So I came up with a little joke to break the monotony. I told the sound man to crank Brown's mic all the way up during his solo. And then, on cue, we all stopped playing and so the only thing people could hear was Brown's fiddle solo. The result was not pretty. Here's how Brown describes it:

"It was so bad, the crowd thought it was a joke and I was making those awful sounds on purpose!"

Brown and I went on to have many greater adventures together. But we still laugh about those times now.

## Cotton, Lloyd and Christian

Early in 1975, I got a call from the music executive Mike Curb. I knew he was a big player in the business, so his call definitely aroused my curiosity. Mike had gained success in the 1960s as a songwriter and producer. He discovered and signed many successful music acts, including the Osmonds. His vocal group *The Mike Curb Congregation* had several hit songs. By 1969 at twenty-three years old he was president of MGM Records and Verve Records. He also signed a young Christian rock artist named Larry Norman to MGM Records.

At that time, Mike had a group signed to his label called *Friends*, which included three talented guys named Michael Lloyd, Darryl Cotton, and Steve Kipner. Michael Lloyd was a successful songwriter and producer who worked a lot with Mike Curb in Los Angeles. Darryl Cotton was a good-looking Australian who was a virtual teen idol in his home country. He had been a member of the popular group *Zoot*, which also included two other musicians who would go on to great careers—Beeb Birtles (founding member of the

Little River Band) and Rick Springfield, who had a very successful TV and solo music career. Steve Kipner was a prolific songwriter and musician who had already enjoyed success in Australia. He would go on to become one of greatest songwriters of the era.

But now Steve wanted to leave the group to concentrate on his songwriting, so Mike needed to find a replacement for him. He decided to form a new group with a kind of international character. He already had an Australian and an L.A. guy. Now he wanted somebody from the American South to round out the group. That's when he called Pat Boone, and Pat suggested me. It was just one more example of Pat's amazing influence on my life, for which I'm forever grateful.

And that's how *Cotton, Lloyd and Christian* was born.

Mike signed us as a new group on 20th Century Fox Records, which was headed by Russ Regan. The label also had acts such as Alan Parsons, disco king Barry White, and the pop band Ambrosia. Soon I found myself walking into a two-story condominium in Beverly Hills, where Michael Lloyd had his studio. I went upstairs and met Michael's recording engineer, a young Chilean named Humberto Gatica. I could tell he was new to the United States, as he spoke very little English. And I spoke Texan. But we communicated pretty well in the studio using hand signals. As with so many people I met in those days, Humberto was at the beginning stage of an amazing music career. Our paths would intersect again years later with two of my most important projects.

By the time I arrived in Los Angeles, Michael Lloyd had already completed most of the tracks we would use for the first Cotton, Lloyd and  Christian album. I also brought several of my own songs, which I'd recorded on 24-track tape with the A Team of musicians in Nashville. We recorded some overdubs and Michael put his finishing touches on them, so they'd blend with the other songs. He was used to recording tracks with near-perfect timing among all the instruments. Hearing the recordings from Nashville, he felt they were a little sloppy. But Nashville musicians went more for the vibe and feeling of a song, rather than accuracy. After recording more music in Los Angeles later on, I better understood where Michael was coming from.

For our first single, we released a cover of the Del Shannon song, *I Go to Pieces*, which had been a top-ten hit for the British duo Peter and Gordon in the '60s. Our version reached number sixty-six on the Billboard Top 100 and the Top 10 on the Billboard Adult Contemporary charts. It was an even bigger hit in several countries around the world.

The 20th Century Records PR team knew how to promote Cotton, Lloyd and Christian, and there was soon a huge billboard of us on the Sunset Strip in West Hollywood. This is a street that's frequently traveled by people in the entertainment industry, so having a billboard there is a smart strategic move. Those billboards are often used to advertise new movies or, as in our case, new albums and recording artists. I have a photo of Darryl, Michael and me standing on the little walkway just underneath that billboard. Gazing up at a gargantuan image of ourselves was a strange experience, to say the least, but kind of cool. I don't think Dow Patterson had one of those in Abilene.

Cotton, Lloyd and Christian began making appearances on the popular music shows of the time: *American Bandstand*, Burt Sugarman's *Midnight Special*, and, in England, *Cliff and Friends*, hosted by the pop star Cliff Richard. We stayed at the Sheraton Hyde Park in London and, this being my first visit to England, I had a hard time adjusting to the food. I ordered lobster for every meal. I figured it's hard to go wrong with lobster, since it's basically just boiled. Johnny Cash's daughter Rosanne happened to be staying in England at the same hotel, and she and I got to know each other. We discovered that we were both from Nashville, so we had a good time visiting.

As we were coming out of the hotel to go to the Cliff Richard Show, we were surprised to find hundreds of screaming girls waiting for us. They started grabbing our clothes as we dove into our car. One of them tore off the right arm of my shirt. I felt I was getting a small taste of what groups like the Beatles experienced every day. It only lasted a moment, but it was a memorable one.

When we did American Bandstand in Los Angeles, the host, Dick Clark, came into the dressing room about an hour before the show. He was very cordial and friendly and began asking questions such as, "How'd you get in the group?" and, "What's Nashville like?" I thought, *Wow, Dick is a really nice guy! He really cares about me!* When we appeared on the show a second time, he did the same thing: "So, what's been happening since you were here last?" Years later, I appeared on American Bandstand for a third time, as a solo artist. Again, Dick came in the dressing room an hour before the show, asking thoughtful questions: "Hey, I know you had some success earlier with Cotton, Lloyd and Christian. What's it like now being a solo artist?" I began to realize what he was doing. Yes, he really was a nice guy, and he really did care about me. But during the show, Dick would always do a little two-minute interview with the artists after they performed. By asking those questions beforehand, he was getting up to speed. It would seem as if we'd stayed in touch since the last performance and the interview would flow as if it were totally natural and spontaneous.

That was Dick Clark—a consummate professional.

## Mike Curb

As part of Cotton, Lloyd and Christian I had the opportunity to work with one of the sharpest and brightest executives in the music industry, Mike Curb. He was a young man then, not much older than me. But he had accomplished amazing things in just a few short years. I learned a lot about the business side from him, which helped me greatly during the rest of my career, especially when I was working out my five-year production deal with Word Records.

When I began my music production and publishing companies, it was Mike's advice that helped me stay clear of the pitfalls that many make starting out. He was also a frenetic bundle of energy, which led to some funny moments. During one of our meetings, Mike suddenly said, "I'm going to miss my plane!" And just like that, he jumped up, left the meeting, hopped in his sports car and drove to the Los Angeles airport. With Mike gone, the meeting adjourned, and I went home.

That afternoon I called Mike's butler, Francis. "Did Mike make his plane?"

"Yeah, he made his plane."

Francis went on to describe what happened. Mike had pulled up at the curb and just jumped out—leaving his car running with the keys in the ignition. Then he called Francis from inside the airport. "Francis, I left my car at American Airlines, Terminal A. Can you go and pick it up? Oh, and hurry. I left the engine running!"

Things were simpler at airports back then.

That was Mike—always on the move, always working, always doing several deals at once. Working with him was never dull and usually successful. But he was a great friend and mentor to me and I'll always be thankful for all he taught me.

Cotton, Lloyd and Christian released two albums, and we had two more hits: *I Can Sing, I Can Dance*, and a song I wrote called *I Don't Know Why You Love Me*. Eventually, we all moved on to other things. Darryl and I continued working together. I produced his solo 1980 album, *Best Seat in the House*, for EMI Australia. I moved to Sydney, Australia for three months while working on his album. Sydney reminded me of growing up in Abilene, Texas—especially when I

got to shop at TG&Y. Most of the musicians on that album were members of the Little River Band. And I contributed some guitar and banjo work. The first single from Darryl's album was a song called *Same Old Girl*, which we wrote together. I was happy for him when it became a number-one hit in Australia.

Michael Lloyd continued as a very successful producer, working with artists such as Barry Manilow, Debbie Boone, Shawn Cassidy, Leif Garrett, and Belinda Carlisle. In 1986 he supervised the soundtrack production for the film *Dirty Dancing*. That included the number-one Grammy-winning song, *(I've Had) The Time of My Life*, sung by Bill Medley and Jennifer Warnes.

I also became great friends with Steve Kipner, the man I was brought in to replace. We had lots of fun times and even wrote a number of songs together, including *Telephone Lines*, which was recorded by Sheena Easton. Steve went on to form the group *Skyband*. He also wrote songs for Janet Jackson, Diana Ross, Neil Diamond, Laura Branigan, the Temptations, America, Cheap Trick, Huey Lewis and the News, and Joe Cocker. A few of his hits were *Hard Habit to Break* (Chicago), *Unwritten* (Natasha Beddingfield), and *Genie in a Bottle* (Christin Aguilera). Steve's decision to pursue songwriting worked out pretty well. Oh yes, he also wrote a song called *Physical*, which became a number-one hit for Olivia Newton-John.

One day in 1984, I answered the phone and immediately recognized Steve's familiar Australian twang. "Hey, Mate! You got a second?" It was a great surprise, hearing from my old friend. "I'm here in the studio with David Foster," he said, "and we just finished mixing one of my songs on the new *Chicago* album." Then Steve held his phone up to the speakers and played the final mix of *Hard Habit to Break*. I was probably the first person outside of the studio to hear it. When it ended, Steve came back on the phone. "So, what do you think, mate?"

"I think it's the best thing I've ever heard in my life."

A lot of other people felt the same way when they heard that song, which Steve wrote with John Lewis Parker. It was released on the *Chicago 17* album, and as a single it reached number three on the Billboard Top 100. It received a Grammy nomination for Record of the Year and Best Vocal Arrangement for Two or More Voices. And it won the Grammy for Best Instrumental Arrangement Accompanying Vocals. What a privilege to be one of the first people who got to hear that masterpiece!

Being a part of Cotton, Lloyd and Christian was a fun experience. It taught me a lot about the pop music business. But, as much as I enjoyed that group, I didn't see myself being in any other groups after that. Now I was eager to take on the next challenge. I knew my future lay in my adopted home of Nashville. But little did I know, my grandmother's prayer was about to be answered in a way I would never have imagined.

# 9

# A Studio Called Gold Mine

Every Christmas, my granddad used to put an envelope in the Christmas tree for me containing a bank stock certificate. As a child, I resented this. Why couldn't he give me something cool, like a red fire truck? Or later, I just wished he might give me a guitar. Or a set of drums. But instead, it was bank stock, every year.

Years later, when I found a house I wanted to buy, that bank stock suddenly became very useful. The home I had my eye on was in Brentwood, about twenty minutes south of Nashville in a neighborhood called Sunnyside Estates. It was an A-frame house on an acre of beautiful, wooded hillside. Best of all, it had a large basement. I needed somewhere to put a recording studio. So, this place seemed like a perfect fit. Apparently, the builder had stopped paying his construction loan, so the house went into foreclosure before it was finished. All I needed to do was put in some carpet, paint the walls and finish out the basement. I went by the bank and offered to buy it for $25,000. I knew it was a lowball offer. But that was the exact amount I'd accumulated in my granddad's bank stock. I was pretty sure I wouldn't qualify for a loan, so that was all I could come up with.

The banker was aghast. "We can't possibly sell it for that!" he said.

"Well, that's all I've got."

And that's where things stayed—until about two months later, when I got a call. "Hey, have you found another house yet?"

"No."

"Well, are you still willing to pay $25,000 for that house?"

"Absolutely."

"Well, come down to the bank and we'll get things papered up."

## A Place to Call Home

And that's how I came into the property that would become Gold Mine Studio. I was looking forward to finally having a studio of my own, and I didn't mind building it myself. But I also had another goal in mind. I knew that Shanon was the woman I wanted to marry. And this house would be a great place for us to live. She eventually agreed, and on May 15, 1976, Shanon and I were married at Calvary Methodist Church on Hillsboro Road in  Nashville—the same church Shanon had attended growing up. My buddy Larry Gatlin sang, Mike Curb and Brown were groomsmen, and I had written a song just for the occasion called *Forever Is Not Long Enough to Love You*. A recording of it was playing as we walked down the aisle after our vows.

After the reception we ran outside through a rain of rice, jumped in the limo, and finally escaped to our honeymoon in Sarasota, Florida. Amy

Grant's parents, Burton and Gloria, had graciously loaned us their beachside home there, and we enjoyed it fully. We took a lot of walks around the beach community, and one day we stumbled on a garage sale. I noticed an accordion for sale—one of the few instruments I'd never learned to play. So, I bought it. And that night, I thought of a great idea. As Shanon was sitting on the bed watching TV, I suddenly emerged from the bathroom wearing my new accordion—and nothing else. Shanon was a shy, conservative Christian young lady who had only been married a couple of days. So, as I serenaded my new bride, she screamed, "Go back in the bathroom! That's gross!"

After our honeymoon, Shanon began getting used to the home she'd inherited, which was basically a '70s bachelor pad until she arrived. It had a brown shag carpet and an avocado green kitchen with orange counter tops. It also had a little loft overlooking the living room that was furnished with a white bean bag chair. I spent many hours sitting in that chair writing songs as I gazed out the window at the beautiful trees of Brentwood.

I dove into finishing out the house and building my studio. I wanted to record demos of the songs I was writing, since I saw myself mainly as a songwriter, not an artist or producer. At the time it didn't enter my mind that I might get involved with Christian pop music. To tell the truth, I didn't even know if there was such a thing. I was familiar with gospel quartets, like the ones I'd recorded with at Monument Studios. But that music was never part of my background. I was from the Church of Christ, where instrumental music was forbidden. Those groups always performed with instrumental accompaniment, so I wasn't exposed to them growing up. I associated them with other denominations, such as the Pentecostals, or, as we called them, the *holy rollers*. I also knew there was some folk and rock music coming out of the *Jesus movement* on the west coast. When Brown and I were in college, one of the records we listened to was *Love Song* by the Christian folk-rock group of that name. I was pleasantly surprised to hear Christian lyrics set to a more modern style of music. But I figured that was an isolated thing, not part of a nationwide trend. So, Christian music wasn't on my radar.

No, my focus was pop music—the music I'd heard on the radio growing up, and which I'd come to love. And that's what I wanted to do. I was a Christian, and that would never change. But I would be a Christian who wrote pop music. That's what was in my mind as I moved into my new house on Sunnyside Drive. But as so often happens, God had another plan in mind, which I didn't see coming.

## Dogwood

Belmont Avenue Church of Christ was situated right on music row in Nashville. In fact, it was there before there *was* a music row. By the time Brown and I began attending in the '70s, the church was in the midst of a revival. The services were so packed that there was barely enough room to stand. Most Sunday mornings there were people sitting on the window sills and on the stage around the pulpit. The minister, Don Finto, was a dynamic, forward-looking man who wanted to reach young people as well as the down-and-out street people of Nashville. So, the church opened a coffee house and bookstore in a building across the street. It was called *Koinonia*, which means *fellowship* in biblical Greek. The church was still affiliated with the Churches of Christ, so musical instruments weren't allowed in the worship service. But across the street, it was a different story. There, talented young believers were free to express themselves with pianos, drums, and even electric guitars. A group called Dogwood became the house band, performing every Saturday night and sometimes on Fridays. They were a trio, composed of Ron Elder and the husband-wife team of Steve and Annie Chapman. When I heard them, I was struck by their original sound and deep spiritual lyrics. At that time, Crosby, Stills and Nash were one of the hottest groups in popular music. Dogwood, with their rich three-part harmonies and innovative melodies, reminded me of them. I got in the habit of going to Koinonia on Saturday nights to hear Dogwood perform. I'd stand at the glass double doors in the back of the room and

just listen. Finally, one day I approached Steve, who seemed to be the main songwriter. "Who's the leader of this group?" I asked him.

Steve, in his modest way, said, "I guess I am, right now."

"Have you ever done a record?" I asked.

"No."

"Would you be interested in doing one?"

"Yeah."

That was a pretty bold proposal, since I had never produced a record and had no contract with any record label. But I did have a plan in mind. I knew that my friend Pat Boone was launching his new label, Lamb & Lion Records, and he was looking for Christian artists with a contemporary sound. He just might be interested in a fresh new group like Dogwood. I called him and said, "Pat, these guys are like Crosby, Stills and Nash—but they're Christian. I'd like to record them."

As he had done before, and would do so many times again, Pat stepped in and gave me the boost I needed. "Well," he said, "how much money would you need to make the record?"

I had no idea how to answer that. I confided that I'd never produced a record, but how about $5,000? Pat said okay. He had never heard Dogwood, but for some reason he agreed to sign them and send the money to produce the record. Knowing

Ch 9. A Studio Called Gold Mine

8/19/72

Dear Chris,

J. E. ate dinner with us today and told us about your telephone call last night. Bless you! I wish you were through with college degree and draft board so you could take up these opportunities. But with your talent, hard work, etc. they will come again. I guess, then the fear of being drafted will cause you to get that degree which, this day & time, is so essential in any field. Pawn to our first grandchild!! We are all So Proud of You! God is answering our prayers, and will for other grandchildren if only they will do their part as you are doing, Prov. 10:4; 13:4, 11. God rewards the diligent, not the slothful.

Love You!
Grand Tida

These are best selling middle-of-the-road singles compiled from radio station air play listed in rank order.

| Last Week | Weeks on Chart | TITLE, Artist, Label & Number (Dist. Label) (Publisher, Licensee) |
|---|---|---|
| 1 | 9 | SHARE YOUR LOVE WITH ME — Kenny Rogers, Liberty 1430 (Duchess, BMI) |
| 3 | 7 | HERE I AM — Air Supply, Arista 0626 (Al Gallico/Turtle, BMI) |
| 4 | 10 | HARD TO SAY — Dan Fogelberg, Epic 14-02488 (Hickory Grove/April/Blackwood, ASCAP) |
| 2 | 12 | I COULD NEVER MISS YOU — Lulu, Alfa 7006 (Moonsung, BMI) |
| 5 | 11 | ARTHUR'S THEME — Christopher Cross, Warner Bros. 49787 (Irving/Woolnough/Unichappell/Begonia, BMI) |
| 7 | 12 | WE'RE IN THIS LOVE TOGETHER — Al Jarreau, Warner Bros. 49746 (Blackwood/Magic Castle, BMI) |
| 12 | 4 | THE OLD SONGS — Barry Manilow, Arista 0633 (WB/Upward Spiral, ASCAP) |
| 10 | 7 | THE THEME FROM HILL STREET BLUES — Mike Post, Elektra 47186 (MGM, ASCAP) |
| 13 | 5 | JUST ONCE — Quincy Jones Featuring James Ingram, A&M 2357 (ATV/Mann & Weil, BMI) |
| 11 | 8 | OH NO — Commodores, Motown 1527 (Jobete/Commodores Entertainment, ASCAP) |
| | | WHEN SHE WAS MY GIRL — The Four Tops, Casablanca 2338 (MCA, ASCAP) |
| 6 | 14 | STEP BY STEP — Eddie Rabbitt, Elektra 47174 (Briarpatch/DebDave, BMI) |
| 17 | 6 | ATLANTA LADY — Marty Balin, EMI America 8091 (Mercury Shoes/Great Pyramid, BMI) |
| 14 | 7 | BACK IN MY LIFE AGAIN — The Carpenters, A&M 2370 (Duchess, MCA/Home Sweet Home, ASCAP) |
| 15 | 6 | TAKE ME NOW — David Gates, Arista 0615 (Kipahulu, ASCAP) |
| 8 | 8 | IT'S ALL I CAN DO — Anne Murray, Capitol 5023 (Chess, ASCAP) |
| 22 | 3 | WAITING FOR A GIRL LIKE YOU — Foreigner, Atlantic 3858 (Somerset/Evansongs, ASCAP) |
| 24 | 6 | ALIEN — Atlanta Rhythm Section, Columbia 18-02413 (Low Sal, BMI) |
| 21 | 4 | I WANT YOU I NEED YOU — Chris Christian, Boardwalk 7-11-126 (Marvia Gardens/Home Sweet Home/Bug And Bear, ASCAP/John Charles Crowley, BMI) |
| 23 | 9 | STEAL THE NIGHT — Stevie Woods, Cotillion 46018 (Atlantic) (Sunrise, BMI) |
| 30 | 2 | WHY DO FOOLS FALL IN LOVE — Diana Ross, RCA 12349 (Patricia, BMI) |
| 25 | 5 | YOU SAVED MY SOUL — Burton Cummings, Alfa 7008 (Shillelagh, BMI) |
| 26 | 7 | FANCY FREE — Oak Ridge Boys, MCA 51169 (Goldline/Silverline, ASCAP/BMI) |
| 27 | 4 | THE WOMAN IN ME — Crystal Gayle, Columbia 02523 (DAS, ASCAP) |
| 9 | 15 | FOR YOUR EYES ONLY — Sheena Easton, Liberty 1418 (United Artists, ASCAP) |
| 16 | 17 | ENDLESS LOVE — Diana Ross And Lionel Richie, Motown 1519 (PGP/Brockman/Intersong, ASCAP) |
| 19 | 18 | NO GETTIN' OVER ME — Ronnie Milsap, RCA 12264 (Rick Hall, ASCAP) |
| 29 | 6 | MEMPHIS |

OCTOBER 31, 1981, BILLBOARD

## Contemporary

These are best selling middle-of-the-road singles compiled from radio station air play listed in r...

| This Week | Last Week | Weeks on Chart | TITLE, Artist, Label & Number (D... |
|---|---|---|---|
| 1 | 1 | 10 | EVEN THE NIGHTS ARE BETTER — Air Supply, Arista 0092 (Hall-Clement) |

---

## Contemporary Christian MUSIC

### THE CCM INTERVIEW
### CHRIS CHRISTIAN
### HIS TURNING POINT

---

# Billboard

The International Newsweekly Of Music & Home Entertainment

87th YEAR

## Cable Blossoming
### Technology Seen As Threat To Radio
By MICHAEL KELLY TUCKER

## INT'L BREAKTHROUGH
### Agreement Reached On Digital Standard
By ALAN PENCHANSKY

### PolyGram Reassesses Mail-Order
By IRV LICHTMAN

### CBS, WEA Seek 'Air' Veto
By IS HOROWITZ

### Top German Pirate Raid
By JIM SAMPSON

---

## Billboard HOT 100
FOR WEEK ENDING OCT. 1, 1977

| TITLE—Artist |
|---|
| STAR WARS MAIN THEME — ... |

## Billboard Top50 Easy Listening

These are best selling middle-of-the-road singles compiled from radio station air play listed in r...

| This Week | Last Week | Weeks on Chart | TITLE, Artist, Label & Number (D... |
|---|---|---|---|
| 1 | 1 | 10 | NOBODY DOES IT BETTER |
| 2 | 3 | 11 | DON'T WORRY BABY |

LUIS
MISED LAND

RCA
APL1-0873

JANUARY 29th, 1976/ISSUE NO. 205

ROLLING STONE

ROLL'S
WHITE

YACHTJACKING:
THE DEEP-SIX
CONNECTION
Murder
and Piracy
on the
High Seas •
A Tidal Wave
of Cutthroat
Drug Smuggling
from Florida
to Hawaii

very-
ut
ly at
ne's
where
e
eeps
I (and
tcy) Away

H FROM
LEY
FALLEN
Legacy:
d Right,
arated Left,
for a King

ALICE COOPER
Breaks the House
at Tahoe

The Divine
Providence of
EARTH,
WIND & FIRE

To Chris
With love
and
Thanks!

The Studios at Las Colinas

CHILDREN

JFK

Produced by Chris Christian

Recorded at the Gold Mine Studios, Dallas, TX.
(▲) All programming and instruments by Chris Christian,
except mix by Ron Jones.
(♦) Engineered by Jack Joseph Puig, mixed by Chris Christian
and Jack J. Puig.
(◇) Produced by Mark Heard.
(○) Piano by Fred Kardt.

1. Father's Grave" (▲) ................................ 2:47
2. Dakota's Theme" (▲) .............................. 2:50
3. Dumon's Song Medley" (▲) ...................... 3:41
4. Walking Across Enchanted Park ................ 4:24
5. Dee Dee Looking For Dakota" (▲ - Newborn) (◇) 3:22
6. Reflection (▲) ........................................ 3:16
7. Climbing To The Top" (▲) ......................... 8:13
8. The Chore" (▲) ...................................... 2:37
9. Acoustic Medley" (▲) .............................. 2:35
10. Father and Son" (▲) ................................ 2:29
11. Casey's Walk" (▲) .................................. 0:19
12. The Glass Rose Parade" .......................... 1:01
13. Warehouse Fire "Dee Dee in Dakota's Arms" (▲) 1:57
14. Soda Shop Medley" (with piano) Wayne Watson (▲) 2:37
15. Only Wanna Be With You" (Chris Christian) (♦) 4:04
                                                        3:07

                                                        3:47
                                                        4:21
                                                        1:00
                                                        0:34

ORIGINAL MUSIC AND SOUNDTRACK
FROM THE MOTION PICTURE

Featuring music and scoring by
CHRIS CHRISTIA
with guests
Mark Heard and Wayne We

LOU DIAMOND PHILLIPS
DAKOTA

TOTAL RUNNING TIME:
APPROX. 43 MINUTES

DVD
VIDEO

*20th Anniversary Collector's Edition*

# DALLAS COWBOYS Legends

This 20th Year Collector's Edition Dallas Cowboys Legends is a must for every Dallas Cowboy fan. Watch and sing along with legendary Dallas Cowboys Roger Staubach, Ed "Too Tall" Jones, Herschel Walker, Danny White, Coach Tom Landry and many others as they sing and present their own special performances of Christmas Classics and other favorites including "Living The American Dream" and "Those Were The Good Old Days." This DVD features footage never before seen on television or DVD. Collect it today!

## SPECIAL FEATURES

Dolby Digital Sound    Interactive Menus    Chapter Search

### INCLUDES

**MUSIC VIDEOS** (Approx. 32 Minutes)

I DON'T WANT TO BE HOME CHRISTMAS
The Dallas Cowboys Alumni '85
TWELVE DAYS OF CHRISTMAS
The Dallas Cowboys Alumni '85
GOD BLESS THE CHILDREN
The Dallas Cowboys Alumni '85
GOOD OL' DAYS
The Dallas Cowboys Legends Alumni
LIVING THE AMERICAN DREAM
The Dallas Cowboys Alumni '86
SILENT NIGHT
The Dallas Cowboys Cheerleaders '86
CHRISTMAS IN DALLAS

**AUDIO** (Approx. 11 Minutes)

"MAN BEHIND THE MAN"
A music tribute to Tom Landry

Tom Landry Interviews:
1. MY FAITH
2. PRIORITIES
3. MY CALLING
4. PREPARATION TO STOP COACHING
5. WHO'S BEHIND ME
6. MY LAST MEETING WITH THE DALLAS COWBOYS

ALSO AVAILABLE ONLINE AT:
WWW.CCENTERTAINMENT.COM

Distributed by:

ymc

www.ymcrecords.com
© & ℗ 1985/1986 LCS Music Group Inc.
FBI Anti-Piracy Warning: Unauthorized copying
is punishable under federal law

*20th Anniversary Collectors*

# DALLAS COWBOYS Legends

Music videos, Christmas
the greatest Dallas Cowboy

*Featuring:* Coach Tom Landry, Roger S
Danny White, Herschel Walker, Bill Bates
Ed "Too Tall" Jones and many mo

*20th Anniversary Collector's Edition*   DVD

# DALLAS COWBOYS Legends

Dallas Cowboys Christmas

what I know now, that was a pretty risky decision on his part—betting on someone who had never produced an album, a group that had never made a record, and a format that was not established. But Pat believed that Christian music shouldn't be different from pop music. He wanted to hear songs about Jesus playing on mainstream radio. That was his inspiration for starting Lamb & Lion. With Pat's commitment, I signed Dogwood to Home Sweet Home Productions and my publishing company. Pat's act of faith in me and generosity would change the direction of my life, and Christian music.

Now, all I had to do was produce a record—something I had never done before. My buddy Brown Bannister and I had been working on the basement studio at my house, but it wasn't finished yet. We needed  to find someplace to record. The Glaser Brothers were a popular country music group who had a studio in Nashville called Glaser Sound. I decided to record Dogwood there. The house engineer was Kyle Lehning, one of the best in the business. Kyle went on to produce hits such as *Love Is the Answer* by England Dan and John Ford Coley, and later worked with artists such as Randy Travis, George Jones, Bobby Bare, Anne Murray and many more. I hired him, and I'm so glad I did. Kyle's expert touch gave the final product a real state-of-the-art pop sound. Without him, I don't believe the album would have generated the interest it did.

Steve Chapman, besides being a wonderful singer and songwriter, was a good acoustic guitar player. And there's something special that happens when a songwriter performs his own songs. So, we had Steve play acoustic guitar on the record. For the rest of the instruments, I wanted the best musicians I could find. I brought in the great Nashville studio play-

ers I had gotten to know during my earlier ventures. We had Mike Leach on bass, Larrie Londin on drums, Steve Gibson on electric guitar, and Bobby Ogden on keyboards along with Sonny Garish, John Rich, and Lisa Silvers. I added some acoustic piano and banjo. With that lineup of musicians and Kyle Lehning engineering, I felt it would make up for what I didn't know, which was almost everything. Producing that album was a fun, rewarding experience. But I also felt pressure to make it as good as possible. Pat was trusting me. I devoted myself to it night and day. I'd stay up till three a.m. listening to each rough mix of the day over and over, making sure the bass and kick drum were perfectly in sync, tweaking this and that.

Finally, we had a finished product that everyone felt good about. And Dogwood's first album, *After the Flood, Before the Fire*, was released on Lamb & Lion Records in August 1975.

## Olivia Newton-John

Around this time, I received a call from a fellow named John Farrar. He introduced himself and told me he was the producer for the pop singer Olivia Newton-John. She was a big star by that time, with hits such as

*Let Me Be There, I Honestly Love You, Have You Never been Mellow*, and *Please Mr. Please.* Many of Olivia's hits had a country flavor, and John Farrar wanted to expand on that by recording her next album in Nashville. It would be Olivia's first time recording in the United States. But he needed a contact in Nashville to help him get things set up. That's why he was calling me. But how in the world had he gotten my name? It turned out that Olivia had a friend named Fleur Theymeyer who was also her seamstress. And Fleur just happened to be the girlfriend of Darryl Cotton, my bandmate from Cotton, Lloyd and Christian. When Fleur heard that John and Olivia were looking for someone in the music business in Nashville, she remembered me. She told John that Darryl's bandmate was from Nashville and knew the musicians and studios there. So he gave me a call.

# Olivia Newton-John

Exclusively
.MCA RECOR

John asked me to make the studio arrangements and pick the musicians for him. I booked a week of recording time at the Creative Workshop in Nashville's Berry Hill district. And I hired Brent Maher as the engineer. As always, I wanted the best musicians for Olivia's project. So again, I brought in the A Team: Joe Osborn, Larrie Londin, Steve Gibson, Bergen White, and Shane Keister. I played acoustic guitar and John would add more electric guitar later.

While John and Olivia were in Nashville they stayed with Shanon and me, and we became good friends. On one occasion we were out to dinner together at Medieval Times, a new restaurant in Nashville, when Shanon began feeling sick. Olivia followed her to the ladies' room, and this sweet international pop star stayed by Shanon's side while she got over her nausea. Eventually it became hard for Olivia to do things in public without being approached by fans. We stopped going out to eat; instead, Shanon went to the market to buy groceries so we could all eat at home.

Many years later I asked Olivia what her memories of those Nashville days were other than the recording sessions. She said:

"You know, the thing I remember most about my visit with you, apart from the fun we had in the studio, it was the first time I'd seen fireflies. I remember being in your garden in Nashville on a warm night and we were sitting on the back-porch steps. There were fireflies blinking all over the garden."

One night John and I retreated to the basement studio and began kicking around song ideas. We ended up writing a song together, *Compassionate Man*, which became one of the cuts on Olivia's album and a single in Japan. That album, *Don't Stop Believin'*, was released in late 1976. It reached number thirty-three on the Pop charts and number seven on the Country charts. And it became one of Olivia Newton-John's many Gold records.

Meanwhile, some things were happening down in Waco, Texas that I wasn't aware of—but would soon change everything for me.

# BJ Thomas

Waco was the home of Word Records, a highly-regarded Christian label that specialized in southern gospel and spoken word recordings. Stan Moser was its head of sales and marketing. I had met him earlier at Mike Curb's house in Los Angeles while working with Cotton, Lloyd and Christian. Pat Boone's Lamb & Lion label had a distribution deal with Word, so Stan received a copy of the new Dogwood album. But he didn't know who had produced it. "It was something very different," Stan would recall later. He was working for a label that specialized in traditional music, but he also had an ear for contemporary sounds. "Dogwood really fit into the musical genre that I was familiar with as a young guy. And so I said, 'I want to meet this guy that produced this album.' And lo and behold, I found out that it was Chris Christian."

So, unbeknownst to me, I was getting noticed at one of the biggest Christian record labels.

Meanwhile, Word Records had signed BJ Thomas to their new contemporary label, *Myrrh*. BJ was a major pop star who had recently become a Christian. Millions of fans already knew his music. He had hit the charts in 1966 with a soulful cover version of Hank Williams' classic *I'm So Lonesome I Could Cry*. He followed that with a solid string of hits: *Hooked on a Feeling, The Eyes of a New York Woman*, and *I Just Can't Help Believing*. His 1969 version of the Burt Bacharach/Hal David song *Raindrops Keep Falling on My Head* reached number one. It was featured in the film *Butch Cassidy and the Sundance Kid* and won the Grammy that year for Best Original Song. And before signing with Word, BJ hit number one again with *(Hey, Won't You Play) Another Somebody Done Somebody Wrong Song*. So, Word Records was very happy to have BJ among its artists. They realized that such a well-known star could help them reach a new, wider audience. And they wanted his record to have a clear Christian theme, but also the contemporary sound his fans would expect. Finding the right producer would be crucial. Jarrell McCracken, the president of Word Records, asked Stan Moser for his advice. As Stan recalls, "I looked at Jarrell and I said, 'There's no doubt in my mind that Chris Christian is the guy to produce this album.'"

So, Stan Moser called me and asked me to produce BJ Thomas's first Christian album. Of course, I said yes. Then I got on the phone to my old friend Brown Bannister. He had been studying music engineering at Belmont University, but hadn't engineered anything professionally yet. "Hey, Brown," I said, "You need to quit that engineering school and come over here. We've got a BJ Thomas record to do!"

GOLD MINE STUDIOS Sunnyside Drive 1974

The next task was to finish our basement studio. We had to put the grand piano upstairs in the living room next to the stone fireplace because there wasn't room for it in the basement. Anyway, the basement door wasn't big enough to fit a seven-foot four-inch piano through. When a song called for an acoustic piano, we'd put a microphone upstairs in the living room by the piano and the piano player would communicate with Brown and me through headphones. But that meant he couldn't see any of the other musicians, which is important in recording.

It was the same when we had to record strings or a horn section. There wasn't enough room for them in the basement, so we'd set them up in a semicircle upstairs with boom microphones. There was Shanon, fixing a sandwich for lunch, with a full string section twenty feet away.

Brown and I worked hard and finally felt ready to record our first album at Gold Mine Studio. And it just happened to be with BJ Thomas, the internationally-known pop star. He was accustomed to working in the best studios in the industry. Ours had decent equipment but was hand-built by novices and funky by any standard. BJ was also used to working with experienced, top-tier producers such as Chips Moman, who had produced many Elvis Presley records. This was only my second effort at producing an album. And it was Brown's first professional job as an engineer.

He was still a little lost sitting behind the mixing console. Musicians would say things like, "Give me another 2dB at 7K" and Brown would have no idea what they were talking about. But he was determined to do things right. He went to Glaser Sound, where we had recorded Dogwood, and wrote down all the equalization settings that Kyle Lehning used. He figured if that's what a big-time professional engineer did, it must be right. Of course, a professional engineer could have told him that EQ settings are adjusted to work for a particular instrument in a particular room at a particular studio. Brown and I were not experienced enough to understand that. We were just doing the best we could with what we had and what we knew.

If BJ noticed any of this, he didn't let on. He came in filled with the joy of the Lord and was totally affable and easy to work with. He gave every song that distinctive BJ Thomas touch that millions of fans had come to recognize. There weren't a lot of contemporary Christian songwriters or publishers, so I wrote or co-wrote most of the songs for the album. Then toward the end of our recording, Stan Moser called and said, "I think I found the hit for the BJ Thomas album." He played me a song by Pat Terry, another Word artist, over the phone.

When I heard it, I said "Yep. You did." It was called *Home Where I Belong*. We had BJ record his own version of it, using the same A Team of Nashville musicians as the other songs on the album.

Now, all the songs were recorded, and I hoped I had finished all the overdubs, so we were ready to mix the album the next day. We worked a long day, so I told Brown to go home and get some rest. We had a big day of mixing ahead. Finally, I went upstairs for a late dinner with Shanon. After that, we went to bed, but I was still going over the day's recording in my head. I dozed off a few times, then about three a.m. I woke up and realized I'd forgotten to add a little glockenspiel bell part to the song. I knew it would really help give it a brilliant high-end sparkle on a walk-down part that was very important to the record. I awakened Shanon and begged her to come downstairs with me. She would be the engineer while I recorded those finishing touches. I showed her where to push the red button to record, the black button to stop, and how to rewind the tape to repeat the process. She was a trooper, and after about thirty minutes the bells were on the tape. We'd be ready to mix in a few hours.

BJ and his wife Gloria stayed with Shanon and me during the recording of *Home Where I Belong*. Many nights while BJ, Brown, and I were downstairs recording, Shanon and Gloria would be sitting upstairs by the fireplace talking into the wee hours. Shanon was always a great hostess and great listener.

*Home Where I Belong* was released in 1976. Within a year it had sold more than 350,000 copies and soon went Gold. That was a staggering achievement for the Christian music industry, where 15,000 sales were considered a great success. It also won a Grammy and a Dove award. Did that little glockenspiel part have anything to do with its success? We'll never know. But I like to think I never let a song out of the studio until it was the best I could do at the time. That song needed those bells! The folks at Word realized they had latched onto a powerful music trend, so they asked me to find more artists to produce. Stan Moser called me and proposed an arrangement in which I would produce five albums a year for five years, which Word would pay for and distribute. At that point, I realized I might just be able to stay in Nashville and make records for a good while, which was why I came there in the first place. I was getting closer to my goal of doing what Dow Patterson did in Abilene! So Brown and I began working to make Gold Mine Studio a state-of-the-art recording environment.

We wanted to do our best and make music that could succeed and be heard on radio stations around the country. And now, with a real budget to work with, we could finally afford the best equipment. I bought a new MCI console, a new MCI 24-track recorder and the best outboard gear of the day. We really had no business building a recording studio to make records. But we were going to need one to fulfill our obligations. Five albums a year was a lot. With all that recording, we couldn't count on being able to book time at the other studios in town. Plus, a producer gets comfortable recording in a certain environment. And it's normal to want to work in one place. Instead of spending all

that money paying for time in someone else's studio, we could put it into equipping our own. It was a better long-term investment. Plus, I was looking forward to waking up each morning, having some coffee, and walking downstairs to work on my records. That was my idea of a creative environment.

**Gold Mine with Amy Grant, Russ Taff and Steve Green**

We hadn't come to Nashville to do manual labor but knowing we could have our own place to make music made it exhilarating and fun. I don't know how many hours we spent working on Gold Mine each day, but we didn't sleep much. I was newly married, and I'm sure Shanon didn't enjoy listening to all those loud hammers and saws in the basement. But Brown was single, so the studio became a convenient second home for him. Once the studio was built and we had a production deal with Word, we worked around the clock to fulfill that commitment and the other projects that came our way.

Brown engineered all my early albums and basically lived at the Gold Mine. He had really become an extended part of the family. Most days after we'd finished our work, he would either put a pillow on the control room floor, or he'd go outside and up the stairs to the house and fall asleep on the vinyl couch. He was in the habit of wearing overalls almost every day and always had a toothbrush sticking out of his pocket. That way he could wake up after crashing for a few hours, go straight to the bathroom and brush his teeth, then start working again. As we picked up more projects, we sometimes found ourselves working on up to nine albums at a time. That hectic schedule continued throughout our early recording days.

Meanwhile, our bedroom was directly above the speakers in the studio control room. They were very large and loud, so that booming sound would be pounding in Shanon's pillow all night. I feel bad about that now. To her credit, she never complained—although I think she might today.

Over the next few years Gold Mine put out an incredible volume of Christian music that included a lot of number one records and many that won Dove and Grammy awards. Some of the most talented artists in the world passed through that basement, and some amazing musical careers were launched.

Left Photo: Pat Boone. Center Photo: Bill Gaither.
Right Photo: Little River Band

For Brown and me, it changed the whole trajectory of our lives. I was now an actual producer—not just a songwriter and instrumentalist. And Brown Bannister became one of the most successful, prolific producers in the history of Christian music.

But at the moment with my new production deal, we were facing a challenge. Who, and what, were we going to record?

# 10

# Amy, BJ, and the Birth of an Industry

The success of BJ Thomas' album, *Home Where I Belong*, marked a turning point for Christian music. It eventually went Platinum—the first Christian pop record to do so. And it made BJ Thomas the most popular Christian recording artist of that time. It was, as Stan Moser said, "a real breakthrough album in *Contemporary Christian Music*. It was really iconic, because it opened the door for, really, a whole new *sound*."

That *sound* was the sound of pop music—with a Christian message. Until then, there had been traditional gospel, Christian folk, even Christian rock and folk-rock. But this was mainstream pop—the type of music you could hear on Top 40 radio, only with a Christian message. A new genre of music needed a new name. In 1978, John Styll began publishing a magazine called *Contemporary Christian Music*. It featured a weekly radio chart of the top Christian music in the nation, so this new genre started being referred to as *Contemporary Christian Music*. Bill Gaither used to have a saying to describe things that were here to stay: "It stuck to the wall." The label *Contemporary Christian Music* stuck.

But as Brown Bannister and I were finishing up the final touches of our basement studio in Nashville, that wasn't on our minds. We had other things to think about. I had just signed a production agreement with Word to produce five albums a year—for five years. That was a lot of songs to find and a lot of music to record. There really was no

*Contemporary Christian Music* industry yet—let alone a reliable stream of contemporary Christian songs, artists or publishers. We needed to find some good Christian talent to sign—fast.

## Amy Grant

Brown had a suggestion. "Well, you know Amy at church—she's got some songs." Amy Grant was a fifteen-year-old girl from Nashville who was attending Belmont Avenue Church of Christ along with Brown and me. She had grown up in Nashville, close to where my wife grew up. Shanon and her two sisters knew Amy and her three sisters. In fact, Amy's sister Mimi was one of Shanon's best friends and had been a bridesmaid at our wedding. And of course, Amy's parents loaned us their beachside home in Sarasota for our honeymoon. Shanon and I thought the world of Amy and the rest of her family.

Amy had written some songs and sang a few of them at Koinonia, the church's coffee house. Brown helped her record a demo tape of two or three songs to give to her parents. Brown played me that demo and I listened to it with a producer's ear. Amy hadn't yet matured as a singer or songwriter—she was only fifteen, after all. But I quickly realized something more important: she was utterly *believable*. Her songs expressed her faith and love for Jesus with simplicity and power. Also, Amy had a natural charisma that simply made people love her. I don't believe she was thinking about making an album at that time. But there wasn't exactly a long line of artists at the door wanting to make Christian records then. So, I called Stan Moser at Word Records. "I've got our first artist to put through our new production deal," I said. "Her name is Amy Grant." I signed Amy to Home Sweet Home Productions, and her songwriting to Bug and Bear Music.

Looking now at the wonderful career Amy has had, it's still amazing to me that *she wasn't seeking a record deal.* Nashville is filled with aspiring artists hoping to "make it" in the music business. But God had a plan in mind for Amy Grant—and it wasn't dependent on her ambitions. As I revisit all that happened then, I have to circle back to my grandmother's prayer. When God answered it, Amy and I were both blessed.

After all, I hadn't come to Nashville to be a producer or a performer. And I certainly never imagined that I would play a role in launching an entire industry. But I've always believed that God orders our steps. The doors He opened for me were doors I didn't even know were there. I keep remembering the Scripture, "The prayer of a righteous man availeth much." I'm not too sure I'm a righteous man, but I've loved Him and I've always prayed. God sure has answered my prayers—along with my grandmother's. The Bible also tells us that *His ways are not our ways.* As others have noted, the Amy Grant—Chris Christian—Brown Bannister connection is a shining example of that.

There was no formula for recording someone like Amy Grant. Brown and I needed some example to follow. I knew of one other singer with a soothing alto voice like Amy's—Karen Carpenter, so I envisioned Amy's first album as a Christian version of a Carpenters record, with that smooth pop sound in all their hits. By this time, I had about nine staff songwriters signed to my publishing company. I gave them all a

challenge: write some Christian pop songs with the Carpenters style in mind. The singer-songwriter Lanier Ferguson had written a wonderful song called *Beautiful Music* that I felt worked well for Amy. That became her first single, reaching number ten. It was followed by two of Brown's compositions: *On and On* and *Old Man's Rubble* (number two), and then, *What a Difference You Made in my Life* (number five). We did include some of Amy's early songs on her first album, but she had not yet become the fabulous songwriter she would eventually become. After all, she was only sixteen.

When we first recorded Amy, we included lots of lush background harmonies like the Carpenters, and "hook licks" like their guitarist Tony Peluso might play. We even brought in the Carpenters' bassist, Joe Osborn, to play on the sessions. I figured every Carpenters-like touch we could get would help create that Carpenters sound. I was technically the producer, but Brown carried the heavy load. Our plan was for me to be the producer on the first record, since I now had a proven track record. Brown would be extremely involved in the production, and then take over from there if the album was successful. And if it wasn't successful, it would mean that I had messed up.

Amy Grant's self-titled debut album was released on Myrrh Records in 1977 and reached number twelve on the national charts. It sold over 50,000 records in the first few months--and kept selling. But of course, it was *My Father's Eyes* on Amy's second album that introduced her to a much broader audience. Those albums would be followed by nearly two dozen more over the next several decades. To date, Amy's records have sold more than 40 million copies, earning twenty-two Dove Awards and six Grammys along the way. And all that from a girl who wasn't seeking stardom! Through it all, Amy has remained the same sincere, down-to-earth person I knew back then. She is one class act, from one great family.

## Dan Peek

Doug Corbin was Pat Boone's son-in-law and head of A&R at Lamb & Lion Records. He called me one day in 1978 and asked if I would produce an album and write some songs for an artist named Dan Peek.

As an original member of the group America, Dan had already enjoyed great fame and success. They were one of the biggest pop acts of the 70's, with hits that included *Horse with No Name*, *Ventura Highway*, *I Need You*, and *This is for all the Lonely People*. Dan had a Christian background but had strayed from his roots in the wake of his phenomenal success. Then, through the influence of his wife, he recommitted his life to Christ. He was eager to share his faith with the world and had signed with Lamb & Lion as a solo artist. Dan came to Nashville for a few weeks, so we could write some songs for his upcoming album.

One morning we were eating breakfast at the Pancake Pantry when Dan opened up the day's edition of the Nashville Banner. The headline read "Malibu fires destroy homes." Dan looked up at me and said, "My house burned down."

I knew Dan lived in Malibu, but his reaction seemed unreasonable. I tried to reassure him. "Aw Dan, your house is okay." But he was certain. He tried to call his wife in California but got no answer. We found out later that the fires had indeed jumped over Highway 1 from Malibu

Canyon and burned Dan's house to the ground—taking his Gold records, his Grammy statue, and everything else. His wife had run into the Pacific Ocean to avoid the flames.

Dan was relieved to hear that his wife was all right. But he later learned the details about his home. He wasn't surprised. The next day I asked him "Why were you so sure your home had burned?"

He told me that when they formed the band America, he got on his knees and said, "Lord, if you'll make this group a success, I will use it as a platform to tell other people about you." But he felt he hadn't lived up to his end of the bargain. With his phenomenal success, Dan had all the material things anyone could want, but he was not happy. Three months before he came to Nashville to write for his first Christian album, he got on his knees again. At his Malibu home by the ocean, Dan told God that he didn't need all these possessions. He really wanted to live his life to glorify the Lord.

And that's why Dan Peek felt so certain that his house had burned down.

It was during Dan's time in Nashville that we wrote *All Things Are Possible*, which became the title song of his first Christian album. Dan and I collaborated on many of the other songs as well. We recorded the album at Cherokee Studios in Los Angeles and the Gold Mine in Nashville. We used the A-list LA studio musicians, I did the background vocals, and Dan sang the lead. The single became the first Christian song on a Christian label to cross over and hit the Billboard Adult Contemporary Top 10, reaching number six. And it was number one on the Christian charts for thirteen weeks. That made it one of the first songs to reach the Top 10 on the Christian and Billboard AC charts *at the same time*. The album was nominated for a Grammy. But ironically, it lost to another album I had produced in that same category—*Heed the Call* by the Imperials. I felt bad for Dan.

## *You* Songs

When we started making Christian pop records I viewed it as a way of reaching as many people as possible with the message of Jesus. But to have the broadest appeal, the lyrics couldn't sound too overtly "religious." Many of them didn't mention Jesus Christ by name but addressed Him as "You." Listeners were free to interpret them as they wished. Some people began calling these "*You* songs."

For instance, the lyrics in the chorus of *All Things Are Possible* were:

> *All things are possible with You by my side.*
> *All things are possible with You to be my guide.*

Christians would recognize the "You" as referring to Jesus Christ. But nonbelievers could also enjoy it simply as an uplifting love song. Debby Boone's version of *You Light Up My Life*, written by Joe Brooks, was another example of this type of crossover song. Some Christians objected to this approach, feeling that it watered down the gospel. But my goal was to reach the world. If the music could be a vehicle to reach lots of people, I was content to let God do the rest.

Still, the objections came, even as the music was gaining huge popularity among believers and the general public. The backlash toward Christian pop artists got particularly ugly when it was directed at BJ Thomas. BJ was a huge pop star who'd had an experience with Jesus Christ and wanted to sing about it. But he also continued to sing his earlier hits, as he had for years. That's what he was known for, and what fans expected to hear when they came to his concerts. But—perhaps because he was such a big star—BJ became a target for some fanatical Christians on the fringe. They came to his concerts and jeered when he sang *Raindrops Keep Fallin' on My Head* and other hits. Sometimes they even threw things at the stage. It was unfortunate. BJ was a new Christian then, and I was disgusted by the way he was treated. I'd like to believe we've come a long way since then.

# The Imperials

One of the stipulations in my production deal was that I would also produce some artists that were signed directly with Word. The first of those was the legendary southern gospel quartet, the Imperials. They had recently signed with the label after some personnel changes and were eager to embrace a more contemporary sound. I had never listened to southern gospel records, much less produced one. The Imperials had a dynamic new lead singer named Russ Taff, who could make an average song good and a great song a hit. But I knew that finding suitable material for them would be a challenge.

Meanwhile, I was scheduled to perform in Clearwater, Florida, so Shanon and I arranged to take a few days off there. When we finally got away, we sat on the beach together, enjoying the sun and idly watched sailboats drifting by.

After a while some words and snatches of a melody began running through my head: *Sail on! When the water gets high, Sail on! When the wind starts to die ...* Within about ten minutes, I had a complete song. I wrote the lyrics down on a Caribbean Gulf Hotel notepad and I decided to present it to the Imperials when we got home. I figured they might think it was too simple, but I played it for them anyway. It wouldn't have hurt my feelings if they had laughed. But to my surprise, they liked it. That left us with only eleven more songs to find—for the album we were supposed to complete in five weeks. We recorded *Sail On*, giving it a little Caribbean flavor to suit the theme, and it became the title song of their album. It was number one for many months and was nominated for a Grammy that year in the Best Gospel Contemporary/Inspirational category.

The Imperials were invited to sing *Sail On* at the 1977 Grammy Awards broadcast, so I flew to Los Angeles to attend the show. I was backstage at the Shrine Auditorium just before they performed and found myself standing next to Bob Dylan. I said, "Mr. Dylan, it's an honor to meet you. I've been a big fan of yours and your songwriting has had a great influence on me." He asked why I was there. I explained that a song I had written and produced, called *Sail On*, had been nominated for a Grammy, and I was there to watch the group perform it on the show. To my astonishment, Bob Dylan began to sing in that famous, nasal Bob-Dylan voice:

> *Sail on! When the water gets high,*
> *Sail on! When the wind starts to die,*
> *Sail on! It's just a matter of minutes till His ship comes to*
> *get us*
> *And we'll all get in it!*

Apparently, even Bob had been hearing the songs we were recording in our basement studio! I never saw him again, but it was not too long afterward that Bob Dylan released his first Christian album, *Slow Train Coming*. Clearly, God had been at work in his life.

And of course, *Sail On* won the Grammy that year.

With the phenomenal success of *Sail On*, there was pressure on us to produce a strong follow up for the Imperials. Brown and I were working on their next album, *Heed the Call*, and found the song we thought could be the next single. It was a tune Brown wrote with Mike Hudson called *Praise the Lord*. As we recorded it, we knew we had something special. Along with Russ Taff's powerful vocal, the piano was the key instrument and played an important role in what became one of the great praise songs of all time. Ironically, that was the same grand piano we had to place upstairs in the living room because it wouldn't fit in the basement.

We recorded all the parts for *Praise the Lord* and began mixing it down one evening about seven p.m. Working into the night, we finally finished about four a.m. We were exhausted. But with great anticipation, we played back what we hoped would be the final mix. And just as the song ended, we heard an earsplitting peal of thunder from outside— right on cue. It was as if God Himself was saying, *That's the mix!* Brown and I stared straight ahead in complete silence for what seemed to be a few minutes. Finally, I turned to Brown and said, "You know, this song is going to last a lot longer than we will." It was a once-in-a-lifetime, magical, time-stood-still moment. And *Praise the Lord* will indeed out-live most of us.

## Becoming a Solo Artist

*Contemporary Christian Music* was now finding its audience, and sales were booming. Brown and I began recording talented Christian artists as fast as we could find them. We needed to turn out a lot of records to fulfill my contract with Word. I thought of one way I could fill one of those five slots each year. I would take the songs I had written that other artists didn't record and make one record a year as the artist. I recorded my first solo album, *Chris Christian*, and to my surprise three of the cuts on it became big hits: *Get Back to the Bible, Great Great Joy*, and *Mountain Top*, which Brown wrote. Soon, I started receiving re-quests to perform all over the country. As busy as we were in the studio, I would slip away on weekends to perform as a solo artist. I still viewed myself mainly as a songwriter and producer, not an artist. I didn't thrive on performing, like my old boss Wayne Newton. Instead, I used those events to gather information from folks I met around the country, so I could be even more effective when I got back to the studio. After each performance I lingered at the record table in the lobby, talking with people and asking questions. *What songs did you like? What type of music do you listen to at home? Who are your favorite artists? Is there any style of music you like that you can't find with a Christian lyric? Do you know of any great local artist?* I wanted to know as much as I could about what our audience was thinking and what types of songs touched their lives.

## The People You Meet on Airplanes

It was on one of those trips that I flew from Los Angeles to Hawaii. Knowing it was going to be a long, exhausting flight, I booked a first-class ticket. And when I found my seat, I discovered that the guy sitting next me was none other than George Harrison of the Beatles. He had a home in Hawaii and was on his way to spend some time there. I got to spend five hours talking with George about music and his experiences with the Beatles. He seemed very interested in the Nashville music scene and the whole world of Christian pop music that was starting to get noticed. We exited the plane and said goodbye, and that was the last time I ever saw George. I always regretted not following up with him after that chance meeting.

On one flight from New York to Denver I met another amazing musician. I struck up a conversation with the guy seated next to me, and discovered that he was Kenny Passarelli, the bass player who had worked with Elton John, Dan Fogelberg, Hall and Oats, Crosby, Stills, and Nash and many others. He played in the group Barnstorm with Joe Walsh, and actually co-wrote *Rocky Mountain Way* with Joe. We became friends and stayed in touch over the next couple of years. Later, Kenny invited Shanon and me to visit him in Aspen and we spent a week there with him and Maxine Taupin, his girlfriend at the time. The entertainment executive Irving Azoff was opening a club there, so we all went to the opening together. There I met Glenn Frey and other members of the Eagles. Glenn and I had a long discussion upstairs at the club that I'll never forget. After all, *Peaceful Easy Feeling* was one of the main songs Chris, Chris and Lee performed at Abilene Christian. Quite an evening for a kid from Abilene!

## Don't Worry, Baby

One day I was walking into a 7-Eleven and heard what sounded like a cover version of the Beach Boys' song *Don't Worry, Baby* playing in the store. I could have sworn it sounded like BJ Thomas! I called BJ and asked him, "Did you ever record *Don't Worry, Baby?*"

"No," he said. "I know the song, but I've never recorded it."

"Well, I think you should." In my head, I was hearing BJ Thomas singing that song with acoustic guitars and a current pop production. I felt if BJ recorded that song the way I was hearing it in my head, it could be a hit.

Meanwhile, Olivia Newton-John and John Farrar were still staying with Shanon and me while they worked on her first album in the States. Mike Maitland, the president of Olivia's label, decided to come to Nashville to see Olivia. We invited him and some other executives from MCA Nashville to a barbecue at our home. As Mike and I talked on the back wooden deck, I told him about BJ and the success of his Christian album, *Home Where I Belong*. And I mentioned my idea to have BJ record *Don't Worry, Baby*. I also let Mike know BJ did not have a secular record deal at the time. A few days later Mike called me. And before long, BJ was signed to a one-record pop deal with MCA records.

We recorded *Don't Worry, Baby* at Gold Mine with the A Team of Nashville musicians. It was released on MCA Records in 1977 and became BJ Thomas' next Top 10 hit. It reached number two on the Billboard AC charts, and seventeen on the Billboard Top 100. It also reached number one in Canada. It's interesting that BJ's version out-charted the Beach Boys original release of the song.

Fortunately, I had the opportunity to work with BJ a few more times.

## MCA Songbird

While I was spending more time in Los Angeles, I received an interesting offer from MCA Records. They knew about my role in the emerging Christian market and knew about the success of artists like BJ, the Imperials, and Amy. Years earlier, MCA had bought a gospel label called *Songbird*, which had become inactive. Now they were hoping to revive it as a contemporary Christian label and they asked me to head it up. I was a musician; I'd never been a corporate CEO. I told them I'd be glad to run the label under one condition—that I didn't have to come to the office for meetings. They agreed, so I accepted. And

that's how I became the CEO of MCA/Songbird. Doug Corbin, one of my good friends, left Lamb & Lion and came over to Songbird as head of marketing and radio promotion.

For our first project, I decided to take the best Christian artists of the day and do a Christmas album. We needed some songs for the project, so for a week I sat in my studio playing with ideas on my Fender Rhodes 88. The title song for the album came out of that effort—*On This Christmas Night*. Also, another one, *God Bless the Children*, which has a hook line that still touches me: "May the Child stay in us all." That's a

timeless encouragement that will always be relevant. I asked BJ Thomas to record it and he delivered one of the most moving, heartfelt, believable performances I've ever heard. He also did a great job on the title tune. Other artists on that album included Reba Rambo, Tennessee

Erne Ford, Amy Grant, B.W. Stevenson, The Boones, David Meece, Mike Warnke, and Dan Peek. It was a real *who's-who* of Christian artists for that time. We also filmed a CBN television special with all the artists performing their songs from the album. What an honor, to work with so many great talents telling a great story!

After that BJ and I began to work on his album *For the Best*, which was named after the first single *"Everything Always Works Out for the Best."* It was released on MCA/ Songbird, as well as a live album, *BJ Thomas in Concert.* They both did well, but not as well as *Home Where I Belong*.

Among the other albums released through MCA/Songbird were several by the group Fireworks, and one by Little Anthony of Little Anthony and the Imperials.

By the late '70s Brown and I were going full steam and loving it. Gold Mine Studio became one of the popular places to record in Nashville, and I had more projects to produce than time to produce them. At one point, almost half of the Top 10 songs on the Christian charts in any given week were records we had produced, performed on, recorded at Gold Mine, or had something to do with. Of course, this was really the infancy of Christian pop radio, and there weren't that many Christian pop releases. But Brown and I were doing our best to produce good quality records, working on many projects at a time.

I remember we often had the great guitarist Dann Huff come in for an entire day to record overdubs. He'd say, "What are we working on today?"

I'd say, "I have no idea."

So Brown would start going through the stack of 24-track tapes on the floor. Then we'd put them on the MCI multi-track machine to decide which ones needed a guitar part. That's what our days were like.

Among the great artists that eventually ducked their heads to enter the Gold Mine basement studio were Bill Gaither and The Gaither Vocal Band, White Heart, Mark Heard, Pat Boone, The News Boys, Larnelle Harris, Billy Joe Royal, Austin Roberts, Nancy Honeytree, David Meece, The Little River Band, Farrell and Farrell, Michael James Murphy, Glen Allen Green, Keith Thomas, and Sandi Patty.

By God's grace, we achieved more than any of us could have dreamed.

Then out of the blue, came a chance to meet Clive Davis and go to Studio 54.

# 11

# Robbie Patton, Clive Davis, and Studio 54

One day I got a call from the music publisher Leeds Levy. He was working with Rocket Music, Elton John's company, and wanted to find a songwriting partner for one of his writers, Robbie Patton.

Leeds was the son of Lou Levy, who had founded the music publishing giant Leeds Music Corporation. Now, Leeds was following in his dad's footsteps, working with Rocket Music and the songwriting team of Bernie Taupin and Elton John, which dominated pop music in the '70s. I had no idea where he'd gotten my name, except maybe he had heard that I'd written songs for Elvis, BJ Thomas and Olivia Newton-John. And of course, I had helped Olivia's producer John Farrar organize her Nashville recording sessions. Anyway, Leeds thought Robbie and I might work well together and wanted to bring him to Nashville, so we could meet. I didn't know Robbie or Leeds, but I thought if Elton John's publishing company wants me to work with one of their writers, I should give it a try.

They both came down to Nashville, and even though Robbie and I had totally different backgrounds, we quickly became fast friends. He's from England, so the culture and atmosphere of Nashville were all new to him. And he found it fascinating. He loved the down-home Southern cooking at Loveless Café and casual breakfasts at the Pancake Pantry surrounded by music people. Robbie and I also discovered that we worked well as a songwriting team. We're both fast writers, so we could turn out a lot of songs quickly. We began writing together for five or six hours a day—between trips to Loveless Café to eat Tennessee country ham and biscuits. The first song we wrote, on his second day in Nashville, was a song called *Darlin*. Before Robbie finally recorded *Darlin*, Darryl Cotton asked me to come to Australia to produce his solo album, *Best Seat in the House*. We included *Darlin* on that album. Robbie later recorded it with the members of Toto playing most of the instruments.

Along with our own songwriting, Leeds Levy also gave us another project to work on. He wanted us to record some demos of hit songs that Elton John and Bernie Taupin had written—with Robbie singing the vocal. Leeds was hoping to pitch the songs to other artists, so they would consider recording them. He felt most artists wouldn't touch a song if he just played them the Elton version. It was too intimidating. Robbie, besides being a great songwriter, is also a first-rate singer, so Leeds felt Robbie would give the Elton songs a fresh perspective.

As Robbie and I began arranging the Elton John/Bernie Taupin songs, it became painfully apparent that although they sounded simple, they really weren't. Bernie would send Elton lyrics in free form, and Elton had a unique way of wrapping music around them that made them flow. It worked great for Elton, but Robbie and I found it extremely difficult to record them again. The songs didn't follow typical songwriting formulas. I gained a great respect for Elton's ability to take random lyrics and make them sound seamless and simple. I had a lot of experience in making demos, but that was the hardest time I've ever had recording a version of someone else's song.

Leeds Levy began pitching our demos to music people on both coasts. As part of his effort to get us exposure, Leeds flew us to New York to attend Elton John's birthday party. It was at a relatively new club in Manhattan called Studio 54. When we entered the club, I saw a scene such as I had never laid eyes on in my life. The disco group Village People was on stage performing and the music was deafening. The room was packed wall-to-wall with people of every description, wearing bizarre clothing—or almost no clothes at all. Looking around, I saw Princess Caroline of Monaco. Andy Warhol. Truman Capote. Rod Stewart. Cliff Richard. Bianca Jagger. Cher. Lisa Minnelli. Brooke Shields. Some of the Kennedy kids. Calvin Klein. Jerry Hall. Debbie Harry. Grace Jones. And of course, the birthday boy, Elton John.

We also ran into the music executive Clive Davis, who had expressed an interest in our music. He asked if we'd like to come to his office and talk about the future. That was intriguing.

Clive Davis was president of Columbia Records and one of the most powerful executives in the music business. The artists he discovered or groomed during his long career include Whitney Houston, Billy Joel, Tony Orlando, Janis Joplin, Barry Manilow, Loggins and Messina, Aerosmith, Pink Floyd, TLC, Rod Stewart, Air Supply, Alicia Keys, Christiana Aguilera, Carlos Santana, Kelly Clarkson, Leona Lewis and Jennifer Hudson. Clive was a virtual star-making machine. He had heard the demos Robbie and I recorded, which included many songs we'd written together. I think he was definitely interested in Robbie Patton as an artist. But I was the co-writer and producer of some of the demos he liked, so he could have been courting us both.

Later that year, Clive called Robbie and invited us to meet with him in New York. Now, we knew he was serious. So off we went to New York again. As we walked into Clive's office he gave us his distinctive signature greeting, "Well, hallo!" Robbie and I always remembered that, and after all these years we still greet each other that way. The meeting went well, and things seemed promising. Then Clive suggested we go out and spend an evening together. We had dinner and then rode across town in Clive's limo to Studio 54. We got out and walked toward the entrance, where there was a black sea of security guards and a huge line of people hoping to get in. Mark Fletcher, the blonde doorman, whom everyone feared, was deciding who could go in and who had to stay outside. Only the famous or beautiful were welcome; the rest were rejected. But when Clive Davis approached, the sea parted, and he walked through like royalty. He paused at the entrance, turned, and smiled back at the crowd and flashing cameras. People were yelling, "Clive, please get us in!"

As we followed him inside, Robbie turned to me and said, "I guess this is the fast lane."

There was the usual crowd of celebrities from the film, music and fashion worlds, all gyrating on the cramped dance floor. It was almost impossible to move. Clive introduced us to several stars, music moguls, and the club owner, Steve Rubell. Then he excused himself and wandered off, saying he'd rejoin us later. After about an hour, one of Clive's associates asked Robbie and me if we'd like to go to the balcony. Robbie immediately said, "Sure!"

Studio 54 was an old theater that had been repurposed as a nightclub. It had several private rooms and quiet bars. It also had an old-fashioned theater balcony.

Now, in Abilene, going to the theater balcony meant taking your girlfriend to do a little kissing. I wasn't exactly sure why we were going

there. I definitely wasn't ready for what I was about to encounter. I found myself first in a line of six people walking up the stairs. When we reached the top, it was very hazy and dark. The black lights created a strange, mysterious atmosphere. As I entered the first row of chairs, I saw what looked like a pile of dust on the small wooden armrests. Instinctively, I brushed some of it off and said, "Doesn't anyone clean up around here?"

I heard a voice behind me scream, "What are you doing?"

Robbie informed me later that wasn't dust.

Clearly, I was a long way from Abilene. Robbie and I laugh about that to this day. And as you might imagine, he's told that story around the world.

Back in Nashville, Robbie and I continued to work together. He developed a close association with the group Fleetwood Mac, touring with them in 1979. He wrote *Hold Me* with group member Christine McVie, which became one of their biggest hits. Christine also pro-

duced and played keyboards on Robbie's first solo album, *Distant Shores.* The single from the album, *Don't Give It Up*, featured Fleetwood member Lindsey Buckingham on guitar and reached the Top 30 that year. It wasn't until Robbie's second album that he recorded many of the songs we wrote at the Gold Mine in Nashville. Robbie eventually decided to sign with another label as an artist, but Clive did remember one of our songs and had his artist, Dionne Warwick, record *"When the World Runs Out of Love"* on her *No Night So Long* album.

After those nights at Studio 54, which were certainly among the most unusual nights of my life, I returned to the calmer environment of Nashville and my work at Gold Mine Studio. But as always, I felt a tug to do more. I've never been one to keep doing the same thing over and over. I learned that while playing for Wayne Newton. My grandmother always prayed that God would use me to reach the world—not just a little part of it. And now, at the height of my success as a producer in Nashville, something was calling me onward to another city—Los Angeles.

# 12

# Can I Swim with the Big Fish?

God had blessed me with a great career in Nashville as a producer and artist. Brown and I were busier than ever, and our music was all over Christian radio. The artists we worked with, such as Amy Grant, BJ Thomas, the Imperials and Dogwood, had broken new ground in *Contemporary Christian Music*. I was well-situated in my adopted home of Nashville. But I knew that the heart of the music business was still in Los Angeles. And I began to wonder, *Could I make it in that world? Could I swim with the big fish?* Without even realizing it, I was responding to an urge inside me to reach the *whole* world—not just a part of it.

I didn't really have many music contacts in Los Angeles. I talked with my mother, who said, "Well, Randy Nicholson's stockbroker lives in L.A. I wonder if he knows anybody there." Randy was a friend from Abilene who I had known all my life. My mom had been his first secretary. His investment adviser was Joe Leach, who worked for Bear Stearns in Los Angeles. Randy arranged for me to meet Joe at his office in Century City. So, I went to Los Angeles with no real prospects—just a curiosity to see if I could compete with the best in the world. I'd had hits as a producer and as a member of a group. Could I do it as a pop solo artist? I wanted to find out. I was always eager to break new ground. God had already given me opportunities that were beyond my imagination—things that *should not have happened*. So why not give it a shot?

In some ways, it was like the time years earlier when I'd driven back to Nashville without any clear job leads. Once again, I was venturing out in faith. But there were differences this time. By now I had worked with the top entertainer in Las Vegas and some of the best artists in the music field; I'd even produced number-one records that won Grammys. I continued to ask God to lead my steps. For some reason, I never doubted that something good was going to happen in L.A.; I just didn't know exactly what.

When I met with Joe Leach in Los Angeles he said, "Well, I don't know if I can help you much. But I have one friend who's kind of in the music business. I handle some of his investments. His name is Robert Kardashian."

## A True Friend

Robert owned *Radio & Records*, a trade magazine for the music industry that provided charts of songs and data for radio stations, which programmers would use in deciding which songs to play. That made Robert Kardashian a very important person, not just to the stations, but to every major record label that needed to break hits. Robert and I met for lunch and hit it off right away. As I discovered, he was not only a warm, genial man, but he also had a deep Christian faith. So, despite his Armenian heritage and my Texas upbringing, we had a lot in common. From that day on we were best friends and enjoyed spending time together whenever possible. And Robert had a great sense of humor, so it seemed we were always laughing. I'm still amazed at how blessed I was to meet a man like Robert. He was one of the people who had a profound impact on my life.

If I was going to work in Los Angeles, I needed a place to live and make records. That need was answered in an unexpected way. One day, John Farrar, Olivia Newton-John's producer, who had stayed with us in Nashville, told me, "Mate, I'm going to sell my home." His house was on Cherokee Lane in Beverly Hills. I had visited him there and knew it would be just right for Shanon and me. It was a horseshoe-shaped compound with a guest house and another bungalow that John had turned into a recording studio. That's where he had written many of Olivia's songs. We recognized the home as a place we could have a base in L.A., and I bought it.

California was a whole new climate and experience for me. After spending eighteen-hour days in the studio for five years, I was so burned out that I ended up taking what amounted to an extended sabbatical. Through Pat Boone and others in the L.A. music scene, we made lots of new friends who shared our faith and values. And we spent a lot of time hanging out together. It wasn't unusual to have couples over for a barbeque. The guys would jump in the hot tub while the wives enjoyed conversation in the house.

Left Photo: Linda Styll, Kathie Lee Gifford,
Suzanne Hayden Right Photo: John Styll,
Ronnie Anglin,CC,Paul Johnson, Tom Hayden

But after six months of being unplugged, I started getting the urge to write again. And in L.A. I met some great songwriting partners. I began working with guys like J.C. Crowley, who co-wrote the number-one hit, *Baby, Come Back* for his group Player; Kerry Chater of Gary Puckett and the Union Gap, who co-wrote *I Know a Heartache When I See One* for Jennifer Warnes; Tom Snow, who wrote such hits as *Let's Hear It for the Boy, Don't Know Much*, and *Love Sneakin' Up on You*; and of course, my old friend Steve Kipner, who wrote almost everything else.

Left Photo: J C Crowley. Right Photo: Steve Kipner

When Robert Kardashian heard some of the songs I was turning out, he said, "Man, that's some really good stuff! You want me to try to get you a record deal?"

"Sure."

But Robert wasn't done. "You want me to manage you?"

"Oh," I said, "I didn't know you were a manager too."

"I'm not! I've never really managed anyone. But this could be fun!"

So that's how Robert Kardashian became my manager. And as it turned out, I was the only artist he ever managed. With Robert's great connections, things began to take off quickly. One of his acquaintances was a young man named Neil Bogart, who had founded Casablanca Records and started the disco trend, signing the Village People, KISS and Donna Summer. Neil was riding high—a bit too high, as it turned out. When Casablanca hit some financial trouble, Neil was forced out. And by the time I met him, he had apparently tired of life in the fast lane. That's when he founded his new label, Boardwalk Records, with the idea of signing more mellow, adult-oriented artists. At that time, soft rock artists like Christopher Cross and Michael McDonald were gaining popularity and Neil wanted to catch that trend. When he heard what I was doing, he liked it. He used to say, "We've found our Christopher Cross!" So I became the very first artist Neil signed on Boardwalk Records, thanks to Robert Kardashian.

Music labels know how important it is to make a big splash with their first release. Robert put me together with the top producer in the business at that time—Bob Gaudio. He had gained fame in the 1960s as one of The Four Seasons, playing keyboards, writing most of their songs, and handling the production and business. After that, he had a much longer career behind the scenes as a producer and songwriter. And he came to public notice again years later with his musical, *Jersey Boys*. When I met him, Bob was at the top of his game, having just produced the Neil Diamond/Barbra Streisand duet, *You Don't Bring Me Flowers*, as well as several other Neil Diamond hits such as *Coming to America*.

So, after arriving in Los Angeles with no prospects, I found myself being managed by a music insider, signed to a major label run by a music legend, and working with one of the best producers in the world. It was another one of those things that just shouldn't have happened. But it did.

## The Amazing Bob Gaudio

Bob Gaudio did an amazing job producing my first album as a pop artist. He listened to the songs J.C. and I had been writing and liked them, so we used the best ones for the album. Bob made lots of minor but complicated modifications that enhanced the quality immeasurably. He also brought in some of the best talent in Los Angeles to contribute: Cheryl Ladd, Amy Holland, Christopher Cross, Frankie

Valli, Tommy Funderburk, Bill Champlin, Carlos Vega, Paul Jackson, Jr., Nigel Olson, Robbie Patton, and Greg Mathieson—just to name a few. I asked Dann Huff to help play guitar on some tracks, which he was kind enough to do. And I introduced Bob to my old Chilean friend from the Cotton, Lloyd and Christian days, Humberto Gatica. He became the mixing engineer on my pop album. His mix gave the album a great clarity and brilliance that still sound great today.

Although I had produced many albums, I was a novice compared to Bob Gaudio, the ultimate pro. I'm still amazed at how much he taught me about song structure and production. His fifty years of sustained prominence and success in the music business were no accident. In my book, Bob Gaudio is one of the great visionaries and music makers of all time.

He's also a wonderful man. We became good friends and ended up spending lots of weekends together with our wives in Palm Springs. Shanon and I have great memories of the fun times with Bob and his wife Judy, who was a strong Christian. After one of our Palm Springs trips, Bob and Judy left on Sunday to go back to L.A. They rounded the mountain where there are a lot of sand dunes, and the wind was blowing fiercely, creating a blinding sandstorm. Judy told Bob they should go back. Bob said, "Don't be silly, it'll be fine." Well, they left in a black Porsche, but by the time they got home to Los Angeles, it was a silver Porsche! The sand had blasted the paint off. We still laugh about that.

We did our recording at Bob's studio in Hollywood, The Sound Lab. During this time, Bob would stay at his condo in Beverly Hills and often we ate at the Hamburger Hamlet, which became our favorite place. During one of those dinners, Bob made a comment that struck me. He said the music business wasn't suited for anyone over fifty. Well, that was before the amazing success of his musical, *Jersey Boys*, which happened when he was over sixty. So I think Bob Gaudio beat those odds.

The album, *Chris Christian*, was released on Boardwalk Records in November 1981. Wanting only the best, Robert hired Gary Bernstein to do the album cover photo. (Among Gary's many famous shots was that iconic poster of Farrah Fawcett that seemed to be everywhere in the '70s.) The first single off the album was a song J.C. and I wrote called *Always Be With You*. Bob Gaudio suggested we change the title to *I Want You, I Need You*. Robert Kardashian booked me on several TV shows to promote the record, including *Solid Gold, American Bandstand* (again), and *The Merv Griffin Show*.

I was accustomed to performing with a guitar, which also served as a kind of prop for me. But Robert informed me that I wouldn't be able to use my guitar on *The Merv Griffin Show*, and that worried him. How would I look onstage with just a microphone in my hand? If I just stood there mouthing words I'd look ridiculous. Robert felt I needed to *move*, which didn't come naturally for me. As it happened, Shanon and I had gone on some double dates with Robert and Kris that involved dancing. And it didn't take a rocket scientist to see I was no dancer. I came from the Church of Christ, after all, where we didn't even participate in high school proms. Instead, we had "Varieteens" which was kind of a senior prom—without drinking or dancing.

"You're about to go on *The Merv Griffin Show*!" Robert said. "You're going to be on national television without a guitar, and you can't dance! You need to get some moves." Before I knew it, Robert had hired a dance instructor to help me out. One morning Robert arrived at my home in Beverly Hills with a flamboyant young man—I'll call him Bruce—who came bouncing into my house to give me my first dance lessons. Bruce listened to the recording of *I Want You, I Need You*, and clearly felt inspired. "Oh, *I want you, I need you!*" he exclaimed. "I love it!" Then he began gesturing broadly to show me how I should express myself. "You just need to reach back into Cupid's love quiver, and grab an arrow, and LET YOUR LOVE FLY!" He shot an imaginary arrow into the air.

I looked at Robert as if to say, *What have you gotten me into?*

Bruce tried to teach me some graceful moves but I'm afraid I wasn't a very good student. After a while I told Robert, "You know, this *love bow* thing isn't really working for me." So, we settled on some more conservative moves, including one where I crossed my legs and did a little spin-around. After some practice, I felt I had it down pretty well.

Robert wasn't the only Kardashian that was concerned about my performances on the *Merv Griffin Show* and *Solid Gold*. Robert knew I needed some moves, but Kris had a better eye for fashion than I did, and she felt I needed to step up my wardrobe if I was going to start doing national TV shows.

As we were shopping, Kris found some grey leather pants, matching zip-up boots and picked out a couple of pink sweaters that all matched perfectly. I'm grateful that Kris was willing to help me spiff up my act. She sure had a great eye for clothes. So, with a couple of new simple moves and my new leather wardrobe, I was ready for prime time.

When I appeared on *The Merv Griffin Show*, I did okay—until it came to my spin-around move. My leg got caught on the mic cord and I stumbled. I would have fallen completely to the ground had my hand not braced my fall. I picked myself up quickly and kept going as if nothing had happened. But there it was. The show was taped for a later viewing—but it was shot live and not edited. So, my stumble was recorded for all the world to see. And that was the beginning and end of my career as a dancing performer! When I appeared on *Solid Gold*, the pop singer Andy Gibb was the guest host, with cohost Marilyn McCoo. She and her husband Billy Davis were part of the popular '60s group The Fifth Dimension. Since then, they both forged strong solo careers, and were strong Christians. Meeting Marilyn turned out to be a great blessing later, as I had the opportunity to make some wonderful records with her.

## Keeping the Faith

Shanon and I were determined to maintain a Christian life amidst the glitz and glamour of Southern California. And as always, Pat Boone remained an important guidepost in our lives. We began attending services with Pat and Shirley at Church on the Way in Van Nuys, where Pat served as an elder. Jack Hayford was the longtime pastor there, and his sermons provided a strong antidote to the shallowness of Southern California life. We got in the habit of going to the Good Earth restaurant with Pat and Shirley after Sunday services. On one such occasion we were all sitting in a booth together. Shanon was nine months pregnant, and suddenly her water broke. We went straight to the hospital where our first daughter Courtney was born. Pat and Shirley Boone agreed to be her godparents.

Pat Boone always kept a strong Christian testimony in the midst of the crazy show business scene. He had many years of experience living as a Christian in L.A.—which I could learn from. In fact, people sometimes made fun of Pat's squeaky-clean lifestyle. And that wasn't just an image; Pat was the real deal. But he did enjoy a good cigar from time to time. I had never been a smoker or a drinker, but during long hours alone in the recording studio, I found an occasional cigar provided a nice diversion from the repetition. So, Pat and I would sometimes drive down to the Tinderbox, a cigar shop on Beverly Boulevard. It offered the finest cigars available anywhere, along with great stories from Charlie, the owner. The Tinder Box was a legendary hangout for the old Hollywood crowd. We often ran into people like actor Roger Moore (James Bond), and spent a couple of hours swapping stories.

Pat and I also enjoyed playing tennis together at the Kardashians' home and the Bel Air Country Club. At one point while playing on the clay courts at Bel Air, we decided to combine our two interests. We began playing tennis while smoking cigars at the same time. It sounds crazy now but made perfect sense at the time. I guess that made us something of a novelty at the country club. One day, we were deep into a tennis game when we heard what sounded like a booming broadcaster's voice coming from the next court: "And, over on the smoking court we have …" We looked over and, sure enough, it was the sportscaster Al Michaels teasing us.

Pat and I were pretty serious about our tennis outings. Even the southern California rain couldn't stop us. Rainy days would find us on the courts, getting soaked but laughing and having a great time. The only downside was that the ball, sodden with water, would go over the net, land in a puddle, and just stop with a thud—like a rock.

Another Los Angeles tennis partner and neighbor was a great friend and mentor, Bob Banner. Like my great-grandfather Lon Christian, he was from Ennis, Texas. He produced many TV shows such as *The Carol Burnett Show*, *The Dinah Shore Chevy Show*, *Star Search*, *Showtime at the Apollo*, and *Solid Gold*. He also won a number of awards, including three Emmys. He gave me an opportunity to be a judge on *Star Search*, hosted by Ed McMahon. And he helped me produce some of the first Christian music videos such as *"Through His Eyes of Love"* by Steve Archer. During the early days of MTV, the only national show that played Christian videos was *Real Videos* on TBN, hosted by Matt Crouch. Bob and I were on the bleeding edge of Christian music videos.

Out of the blue I got a call from the legendary Barry Gordy to come play tennis at his Bel Air home. As he came to the front door to meet me, the first thing he said was "You can take your shoes off and leave them inside at the front door". As I entered his spacious home barefoot with my tennis bag, the artist Charlene was there. Barry wanted me to write some songs and produce some demos for his artist Charlene. She recently had a #3 Top 100 song *I've Never Been to Me* that also reached #1 in many other countries. We did, however, record a Christmas duet, *Christmas All Year Round*, that is still played on radio today. Although I thought it a little unusual to have to take my shoes off to enter the house, it was fun to play tennis with Mr. Motown.

Meanwhile, *I Want You, I Need You* reached number six on the U.S. Billboard Adult Contemporary (AC) charts and number thirty-seven on the Billboard Top 100. It hit number one in many cities and in other countries such as the Philippines. We followed it up with a cover version of the Motown hit, *Ain't Nothing Like the Real Thing*. Our version was a duet with Amy Holland, who later married Michael McDonald. It also reached the Top 10 on the Billboard AC charts. Robert and I wanted *What Can There Be* to be the next single, but Neil preferred *Make It Last*, which was a more rock-oriented tune. He was concerned that I'd be pigeonholed as a ballad singer. Also, Neil had recently signed rock acts Joan Jett, Ringo Starr and Night Ranger, and he wanted to take the label more in that direction.

*Make It Last* was moving up the Billboard charts when Neil passed away from cancer at the young age of thirty-seven. He had been the driving force behind Boardwalk as well as my pop career. The label began a rapid decline after his death, eventually filing for bankruptcy. From all this tragedy, one good thing happened. Robert arranged for me to regain the ownership of my Boardwalk album, my publishing, and all related assets. It was probably my best recording, so I was glad to add it to the other Christian albums I owned. Since then, lots of commenters have noted that Neil missed another hit by not releasing *What Can There Be*. My good friend Robbie Patton sang on it, adding a great vocal texture in the fade. Who knows what might have happened if Neil had taken Robert's suggestion? Maybe one day we'll find out.

With Neil's death, my career as a solo pop artist was effectively over. But I had proved that I really could swim with the big fish. More importantly, I had formed many valuable relationships in Los Angeles that would last far into the future—and some of those friends would become known around the world.

# 13

# Hanging with the Kardashians

Robert Kardashian introduced me to a whole new phase in my music career. But he wasn't just my manager. He also became my best friend. We found an immediate bond in our shared Christian faith. Beyond that, he was just a kind and decent human being.

He also loved a good joke. One Sunday Robert and I were attending the Vineyard church in West Los Angeles, which was often attended by celebrities. It wouldn't be unusual to look around and see Bob Dylan, Keith Green, Bernie Leadon of the Eagles, Priscilla Presley, Debby Boone, Lisa Whelchel or Tommy Funderburk sitting in the next pew. Shortly after the service began, a fellow with long blonde hair came in and took the empty seat beside us. I looked at Robert as if to ask, *do you recognize him too?* He nodded. It was the actor Jeff Bridges. Meanwhile, the pastor, Ken Gullickson, launched into a sermon about the perils of wealth. He quoted Matthew 19:24: "It is easier for a camel to go through the eye of a needle than for someone who is rich to enter the kingdom of God."

"Look around you!" Pastor Ken said. We all began looking at each other, not sure where he was going with this. "Look at the cars in our parking lot. Most of you are wealthy! According to this Scripture, very few of you are going to hear the trumpet of the Lord when He comes!"

A minute later, with perfect timing, Robert looked over at me and Jeff Bridges and whispered, "Did you guys hear that trumpet?" Of course, we broke up laughing. But that was Robert—always light-hearted and joyful, in a mischievous kind of way.

It is said that there are fewer Christians per capita in West L.A. and Beverly Hills than in Japan. Christians in the entertainment business know that declaring their faith openly can hurt their careers. They naturally gravitate to other believers for support. Recognizing that need for fellowship, Robert began hosting a Bible study at his home in Bel Air along with the actor Stephen Shortridge, who was known for his role in the TV series *Welcome Back, Kotter*, and Tommy Funderburk who was one of great singers of that time. Those regular meetings, often taught by Ken Gullickson, became a refuge for Christians in the music, film and TV industries. That was typical for Robert. His commitment to God was genuine and never wavered during all the years I knew him.

Robert liked to eat too, as did I, and we often went to dinner together. He introduced me to the Cheesecake Factory and the Mandarin in Beverly Hills, which later became the popular chain P.F. Chang's. These were our go-to places, and they remain my two favorite restaurants today. I can't walk into either one without thinking of Robert.

One night he took me to The Roxy, the popular Sunset Strip rock club, to hear Christopher Cross perform. Robert thought I might like to meet Christopher, since he was a fellow Texan from Austin. Christopher was at the peak of his popularity  then, following the success of his songs, *Ride Like the Wind* and *Sailing*. After the show we went backstage to visit with him and his manager, Tim Neece, who is also a fellow-Texan.

After moving to L.A., it wasn't long before I found myself surrounded by some of the top people in the music business. It made me think back to Mrs. Patterson's fourth-grade class in Abilene, and how I'd set my heart on a life in music all those years ago. And now, here it was! That period in Los Angeles was probably the pinnacle of my career as an artist. But there were many more musical adventures yet to come.

David Foster, Tommy Funderburk, Chris, Jay Graydon, Steve Lukather

## Family Times

Getting to know Robert meant getting to know his family. The Kardashians have become famous in the years since then, with their reality TV show, *Keeping Up with the Kardashians*, and their various public activities. But Shanon and I got to know a different side of them. At that time, Robert and Kris were a charming young married couple with three adorable little children, Kourtney, Khloe', and Kimberly, (as we knew her then). Rob Kardashian was born later in 1987.

The Kardashians became like family to us. Kris and Shanon were inseparable—so much so that when our second daughter Casey was born, Kris was there in the delivery room at Cedars-Sinai filming it. At the baby shower for our first daughter, Courtney, one of our guests was Kathie Lee Johnson (later Gifford), who met Kris Kardashian there for the first time. It was the beginning of their long friendship. Kris was also responsible for introducing Shanon to Community Bible Study (CBS), and she has always appreciated Kris making that introduction. Shanon still attends CBS in Dallas.

Those early days were filled with fun activities between our two families—Christmas, Thanksgiving, birthdays, charity softball tournaments. And Robert always involved his close friends in whatever he did. One of those friends was his old college roommate from USC, with whom he'd stayed close over the years. His name was O.J. Simpson. As a water boy for the USC football team, Robert had witnessed O.J.'s phenomenal career from the beginning. And later, after Robert became a lawyer he helped O.J. negotiate his first contract in the National Football League. O.J. and his wife Nicole were often there at Kardashian family functions.

Robert was a loyal USC alumnus, so we often went to USC football games together. On one occasion, O.J. came with us. As we stepped out of the car at L.A. Memorial Coliseum, a crowd of people quickly formed around O.J. asking for his autograph. I don't think they even noticed Robert or me. After signing a few autographs, O.J. looked up and told Robert and me to go ahead; he'd join us later. We went inside and took our seats. The game began, but O.J. hadn't arrived yet. It continued to the middle of the fourth quarter—still no O.J. Then suddenly we saw a mob of people emerging from the tunnel, heading to where Robert and I were sitting. It was O.J. and his crowd of admirers. He was still signing autographs! I think he granted every single request before he finally sat down with us to watch the last few minutes of the game. That was the level of fame that O.J. Simpson lived with every day back then.

Later, when my family was in Texas, Kris and Robert's oldest daughter Kourtney was trying to decide which college to attend. She wanted a

USC-type education like her dad, but also wanted to go somewhere outside of California. Robert called me one day and said Kourtney had decided to attend the "USC of the south," Southern Methodist University in Dallas. He asked if I would help her move into her new apartment, which was in the Knox Henderson area, close to SMU. Robert had rented some furniture for her, so after I gave them a tour of the area, Robert and I carried her furniture up to her second-floor apartment. Neither one of us was very good at manual labor, but after a few mishaps, we got her settled. I was hoping Kourtney would love Texas as we did and become an adopted Texan, but after two years at SMU she decided Texas was not her style. But that short period when Robert stayed with us gave me some time to show him around Dallas and let him see my little part of the world.

## The Dark Days

Those were fun days, but things later took a very dark turn. In 1994 Nicole Simpson was murdered along with Ron Goldman, and her ex-husband O.J. was charged with the crime. Robert famously stuck by his friend and even helped to orchestrate O.J.'s surrender to the police. The day before his arrest, O.J stayed overnight at Robert's house. As it happened, I came into town from Dallas the very next day after O.J. surrendered. In those days I always stayed at Robert's house when I came to Los Angeles. So I ended up spending the night in the same bedroom where O.J. had stayed the night before. It was a very eerie feeling.

Robert, being a well-connected attorney, helped O.J. assemble his famous "dream team" of lawyers and worked with them to plan a defense strategy. By Christmastime, everyone involved with the case was ready for a break. Robert invited me to a Christmas party at his home in Sherman Oaks. When I arrived, the entire defense team was there, along with many of Robert's friends. David Foster, the producer and composer, came with songwriter Linda Thompson (whom he later married). Linda had been close with Elvis, so I already knew her from the Memphis days. Warren Wiebe, a popular studio vocalist, was also there. He sang a selection of Christmas songs while David Foster accompanied him on the electric piano in Robert's grand room. It was a welcome moment of hope and light in a very dark time.

I stayed with Robert for a few days after that. One night we were ready to go out to dinner and he told me, "I hope you don't mind; I've got another guest coming. I couldn't get out of it." Of course, I agreed. When we met at a Beverly Hills restaurant, I found out that the other guest was the attorney F. Lee Bailey. I didn't say much as they spent the next several hours discussing O.J.'s defense strategy. But I was all ears.

The media became obsessed with the O.J. Simpson trial and anyone associated with it was a subject of interest. As one of O.J.'s best friends, Robert Kardashian was a particular target for attention. Meanwhile, some tabloid publications found out I was Robert's friend, so I began receiving offers of $20,000 and $30,000 to provide "dirt" on him. My response was "Well, you can give me $30,000 if you want. But I have nothing bad to say about Robert Kardashian. And I wouldn't tell you if I did."

That was the truth. There was simply nothing bad to say about Robert. He was a prince of a man, all the way to the end.

During this time Robert and I talked on the phone almost every day late in the evening. He would tell me about the day's activities, and I heard an inside view of things that most people weren't exposed to. People who know about my connection to Robert often ask me, "So, did he think O.J. was guilty?" The truth is—I never asked him. It was just too personal, too sensitive. But it's no secret that as the evidence against O.J. began to mount, Robert became very concerned. Meanwhile, there was tremendous pressure on him to abandon O.J. But, being a person of integrity, Robert felt it was right to stand with his friend and let the system do its work. In the end, O.J. was acquitted of murder. And Robert suffered greatly, personally and professionally, for his loyalty. He was ostracized. He received death threats. His personal life was disrupted.

In the years that followed, Robert's public statements about the trial were always careful and guarded. But a glimpse of his true feelings can be seen in the now-famous video clips of the moment the verdict was announced. At the words "not guilty" O.J. and his attorney Johnny Cochran broke into jubilant celebration. But standing right next to them was Robert Kardashian. He looked nauseated. To me, the most accurate look into Robert's heart is how he signed his note to Shanon and I inside the book, *American Tragedy*.

*"Follow Truth wherever it may lead".*

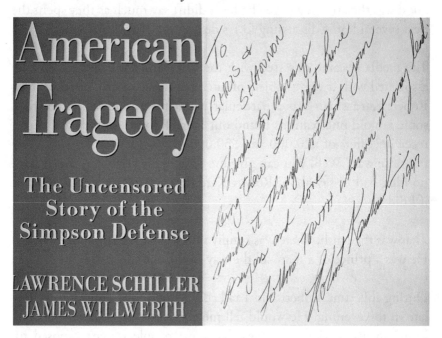

When Robert sold his record business tip sheet, *Radio & Records*, he hatched an idea for another business. He called it *Movie Tunes*. He would arrange with theater chains to play music for thirty minutes before their movie trailers began. And then, using his many relationships in the music business, he sold that time to the record companies, so they could gain exposure for their new record releases. Robert always wanted his kids to be productive and successful, and he looked for opportunities to involve them in his business activities. Kim was older now, so he gave her a part time job at Movie Tunes. One day I visited Robert at their office in Sherman Oaks. And there was Kim, sitting in front of a computer with her Gucci purse, doing her nails. I said, "Hey, Kim. What'cha up to?"

"Oh, just doing my nails."

I glanced up at Robert, who gave me a puzzled look. As we walked out to go to lunch, he said, "I wish she could find a way to make a living with her fashion!"

In 2006, Kim and her sister Kourtney opened a boutique clothing and accessory chain. I was amused that they decided to name it *DASH*—which had always been my nickname for Robert.

In 2003 I received a call from Robert Kardashian's brother Tom who was in Dallas at a business meeting. "I'm at the Four Seasons hotel," he said. "I need you to come out. It's very important." When I met with Tom, he told me that Robert was in very poor health. He was later diagnosed with esophageal cancer. And within a few weeks, he was gone. That day I lost a big part of my life. But I still feel deeply honored and grateful to have had Robert Kardashian in my life. Today, Shanon and I remain good friends with Kris and the kids. The public sees their flamboyant side; we see a family that loves each other. And we see Kris devoting much of her time and money to church and charitable causes. We remember her as the loyal, consistent, sweet friend who introduced Shanon to Community Bible Study.

## Ready to Move

Getting to know the Kardashians was just one of the blessings that came our way in Los Angeles. We had met great people like Bob and Judy Gaudio. I had worked with or written for artists such as Natalie Cole, Sheena Easton, Olivia Newton-John, the Pointer Sisters, Al Jarreau, The Carpenters, Patti Austin, Gerry Beckley, America, Deniece Williams, Marilyn McCoo, Dan Peek, Dionne Warwick, Donnie Osmond, Cheryl Ladd, Amy Holland, Pat Boone, Andrae' Crouch, B W Stevenson, Little Anthony, and J.C. Crowley of Player. But I always knew that Los Angeles would not be my permanent home. Being a Texas boy, I always found the L.A. culture somewhat foreign. I noticed that people seemed very high-strung and paranoid. As I learned more about the L.A. business environment, I understood why. Everyone was afraid of being ripped off!

In Los Angeles, everyone wants to be seen driving a nice car and living in a nice home—even though some can't afford it. In Texas, we'd describe that as *all hat, no cattle*. Among Texans, it's not considered cool to flaunt one's wealth. You're more likely to see a wealthy person wearing jeans and driving a pickup truck or an old car.

And of course, everyone knows about the decadent side of L.A. Oddly enough, I'd always heard about the prevalence of drugs—especially cocaine. But I never saw drugs being used while I was there, and no one offered me any either. I wouldn't have been interested anyway. But I guess God was still protecting me—and answering my grandmother's prayers.

Los Angeles was not where Shanon and I wanted to raise our kids. Knowing this, I had moved my office to Dallas when we bought our home in Beverly Hills. That way, when the time came to move back to Texas, I'd already have my office there. I also told my brother, who lived in Dallas, to keep an eye out for a property I could buy there. I wanted something in the *Golden Triangle* area between Dallas, Denton and Fort Worth that would appreciate in value over the years. One day Brad called me and said, "I found what you're looking for." It was a fifteen-acre mini-ranch in Argyle, north of Fort Worth (quarter horse country). He said I'd better fly back and look at it immediately, since it wouldn't stay on the market long.

I was in the middle of several album projects, but I arranged to take a midnight flight from Los Angeles to Dallas. Brad picked me up at the DFW airport at seven a.m. and we drove straight to the property. The owner was there in his Wrangler jeans, cowboy hat and cowboy boots—a true Texas rancher. Meanwhile, I showed up wearing a funky Hawaiian shirt and some pink tennis shoes Nike had given me for a TV show—pure California.

The old rancher looked me up and down, and said in his Texas twang, "Well, what we got here?"

By ten a.m. I said, "I'll take it," and Brad took me back to the airport. I was back in Los Angeles for my two-p.m. recording session.

I held on to that property, knowing that at least it would be appreciating in value while I waited for the right time to move. Now, it seemed that time had arrived. At the height of a music career that was going strong in California, I began feeling that tug inside again.

Texas was calling.

# 14

# Home Where We Belong

"Well, it's eight a.m., about time to get ready for church!"

It was the familiar, legendary voice of Ron Chapman, Dallas's premier radio D.J. My car radio was tuned to KVIL, the top pop station in Dallas.

*Yep*, I thought, *I'm home.*

I wouldn't have heard anything like that on a Los Angeles radio station. Christians are a minority in L.A. Being Christian there is considered odd—just as it would be odd to be an atheist in Texas. And despite all the great experiences I'd had in Los Angeles, I always knew I'd move back to Dallas someday. Over the previous decade, God had allowed me to fulfill my fourth-grade dream—to make music and have a hit on the radio like Dow Patterson. Now, after more than a hundred songs on the Christian charts and seven Billboard Top 10 records, it was time to focus on raising my family. Shanon and I now had two preschool-age girls, Courtney and Casey. We wanted them to grow up in a healthy environment, away from the ruthless materialism that's so common in L.A. In Texas, people are genuinely nice—not just when they have something to gain. And neighbors genuinely care about each other. It's hard to tell who's wealthy in Texas because people understate their wealth—in contrast to L.A. where image is everything. Texans care about who you are, not how you appear.

I was grateful that we had a place to live while we searched for the perfect home. Of course, I was still going to make music, so we needed someplace where I could put a recording studio close to our home. At this stage of life, I needed to be able to work long hours in the studio—but still be close for my young children at mealtimes and other important occasions.

We found a new home that was almost completed on Meadow Road in an area of Dallas called Preston Hollow. We loved it and decided to buy it. We also purchased the older home next door, which I could use as my recording studio. We put in a pool, fence and gate, turning both properties into a small compound with lots of land where our kids could play. Shanon did most of the heavy lifting to finish our new home while I spent my time building the studio next door. It seems I couldn't go one day without having a studio to work in. That became my third studio, after Gold Mine in Nashville and our studio in Beverly Hills. Some great music came out of that Texas studio, including many number one Christian records. I produced and recorded Steve Archer, Eric Champion, B.W. Stevenson, Jeffery Smith, Mike Eldred, and Luke Garrett, along with many other artists. As time allowed, I also recorded what I think are some of my own best records such as *Day Like Today, Focus On the Child, Don't Blame It On the Ones You Love*, and two instrumental albums: *No Lyrics* and *Sketches*. I flew in the best musicians from Nashville for overdubs—such as my favorite guitarist, Dann Huff. I still traveled to Nashville and L.A. as necessary for dates, and I continued to perform around eighty concerts a year as an artist.

But at last, I was living back in my home state of Texas. It felt great.

## Making Music for Sports Television

Lance Barrow was an executive producer of golf and football events for CBS Sports. One day he was in the lobby of a hotel in Atlanta when he heard one of my songs. He called the radio station to find out who the artist was, and to his surprise, they told him it was Chris Christian. When he called I found out he is an alumnus of Abilene Christian College and was also a member of the Church of Christ, so we had a lot in common. Then he told me why he was calling. He wanted me to write and produce the music behind the opening seven minutes of the upcoming Masters broadcast. It was a new opportunity and of course I took it.

Lance sent me the edited video footage of the show's opening on three-quarter inch video tape with time code. He told me where he wanted certain types of music and I worked for a week trying to meet his expectations. Then I sent it off to him in New York.

Lance called me, and said in his gruff voice, "You know that segment starting at four minutes and ten seconds and ending at four minutes fifty-two seconds? It needs to be more up-tempo, more intense. Can you fix that part?"

"Sure," I said, "when do you need it?"

Lance said, "Look out your window. Do you see a delivery truck?"

I walked over and looked out the window. Sure enough, there was a delivery truck.

"When you're finished, walk out the front door of your studio and give it to him," Lance said. "He's taking it to the airport. I have a plane waiting to fly it to me in New York."

Of course, those were the days before FedEx or the Internet. But that's the kind of effort Lance would make to get the music right in his sports broadcast. It's my belief that his attention to the music underneath the visual was a large part of why CBS had the best sports broadcast on television in those days. I was now in an interesting new phase of my music career, writing and producing music for The Masters golf tournament, The Super Bowl, the NCAA finals, the Olympics, and the U.S. Open tennis tournament. That lasted for several years.

## Dakota

Making music for television was exciting, but then a whole new creative opportunity came my way—movie soundtracks. The Kuntz brothers were a couple of Dallas-based filmmakers who were shooting a film called *Dakota*, starring the known, but not yet mega-star, Lou

Diamond Phillips. When they heard I'd moved to Dallas they contacted me to ask if I would write and produce the soundtrack. Over the years, some of my songs had been used in movies, but I'd never been solely responsible for all the music and scoring on a major film. Of course, I said yes.

Over the next six months, I attended dailies with the cast and I'd receive segments of the film as they were edited. Then I wrote and produced music to complement what was on the screen. I learned that one of the trickiest things about scoring a film is to enhance the emotions of a scene while staying just below the audience's conscious awareness. The process was very educational and rewarding for me. Lou Diamond Phillips, of course, has had a long and distinguished acting career. And I later released most of the Dakota music on my album *Sketches*.

## Frank and Kathie Lee

Football is a big part of life in Texas. So, I was excited and surprised when I got a call one day from a football legend.

"Is this Chris?" the voice asked.

"Yes."

"This is Frank Gifford."

At first, I thought it was one of my friends playing a joke. But no, it really was Frank Gifford, the Pro Football Hall-of-Famer and sportscaster. It turned out that Frank was courting Kathie Lee Johnson and wanted to get to know some of her close friends. So, he invited me to come and visit him at the Monday Night Football broadcast booth at Texas Stadium that Monday—and possibly meet him at the Four Seasons after the game. When the day came, I picked up the tickets and passes he had left for me at the Four Seasons, went to the game, and walked up to the booth to meet Frank for the first time. What a thrill it was for this Cowboys fan to spend time with Frank and his fellow sportscaster Al Michaels. Frank and I had a nice talk during halftime and I found him to be friendly and charming. After that, we did get together at the Four Seasons. It always struck me how thoughtful he was to reach out to Kathie Lee's friends like that. Frank and Kathie Lee eventually married, of course. Shanon and I attended their wedding and spent time with them at the Grammy Awards and their Connecticut home.

We moved back to Texas for family reasons. Dallas wasn't known as an entertainment hub, so I wasn't sure what I would do there. But far from being quiet and sedate, our life in Dallas was proving to be lively and busy. I was finding new opportunities I would never have had in Nashville or California. Then, out of nowhere, one call opened an opportunity that would give me a brand-new challenge outside of music.

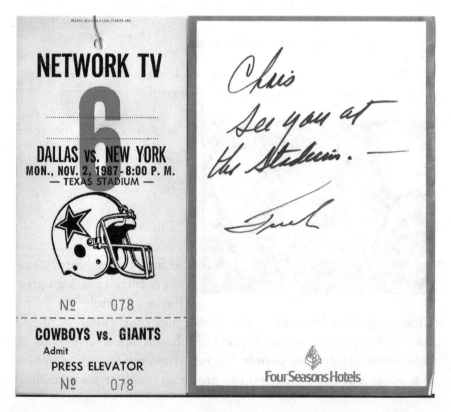

# 15

# The Movie Studios

Don Williams was a close friend from the Church of Christ who served as a trustee at Abilene Christian University and was also godfather to Casey, one of my daughters. So, when he invited me to his real estate office one day in 1992, I was eager to go—and curious too. "I have something I'd like to talk with you about," he said. Don was the CEO and chairman at Trammel Crow, one of the largest real estate development companies in the world. I wondered what he might have in mind. After all, I was a music guy with little experience in real estate.

I drove to Trammel Crow Center, a fifty-story skyscraper in downtown Dallas. Since Don was the CEO, I was expecting to meet him in a spacious corner office. Instead, I was surprised to find his office in the middle of the floor with everyone else's, with a regular desk just like all the other desks. That was Don—nothing flashy or pretentious. After we exchanged greetings and small talk, he began to tell me about a property they were planning to sell. It was a movie soundstage in Irving, Texas northwest of Dallas, called *The Studios at Las Colinas*. And he was wondering if I'd be interested in buying it before they put it on the market. I knew nothing about owning a movie studio, but I was intrigued.

The Studios were the vision of Trammel S. Crow, son of the founder, Fred Trammel Crow. His plan was to build a movie complex and for Texas to become a third coast of film production. The Studios, a 72,000 sq. foot building with 3 soundstages, were built in 1981 for $12 million. It was part of a huge project that came to be known as the Dallas Communications Complex. Most of the development consisted of commercial office buildings, which was really Trammel Crow's core business. The company didn't know what to do with the movie studios, so now they were going to put it up for sale. Don didn't know anyone else in the entertainment business, so he called me.

I spent the next month consulting my most trusted friends; doing research; diving into the numbers, projections, and ongoing obligations of the property. And I decided to go for it. This would be a very complicated transaction, so I brought in a partner who understood the real estate details better than I did. This was going to be the first time I would need a loan for more money than I had. Normally I wouldn't have qualified for such a large loan, but my friend Ty Miller and his wife Jan were godparents to our daughter Savannah. Ty was also president of Bank One. He stepped up and authorized the loan. It was a bold move on his part. And it turned out to change my life and my family's life forever. I'll always be grateful to Ty.

With the largest soundstages outside of California or New York, The Studios were a popular location for film shoots. The feature films shot there included *Robocop*, *JFK*, *Born on the Fourth of July*, *Leap of Faith*, *Silkwood*, and *Terms of Endearment*. TV shows included *Barney & Friends*, *Dallas*, and *Walker, Texas Ranger*. A lot of commercials were shot there as well.

Stage A was a soundproof, 15,000-square-foot space where big-name music acts came to rehearse and shoot videos. It offered the security and seclusion they needed and all the space they could want. So, at various times, Eric Clapton, Phil Collins, Stevie Wonder, Willie Nelson, Julian Lennon, the Everly Brothers, Garth Brooks, Leon Russell, and ZZ Top came through. It occurred to me that the public might enjoy getting a glimpse of this amazing place. I remembered how successful the Universal Studios tour in Los Angeles had been. While I was living in L.A., I had worked at the MCA/Universal Records building right next to the Universal tour, and I often heard people say that the tour generated more money than the films themselves. Not all movies are profitable. But at the Universal Studios tour, people would line up every day and pay good money to tour the backlots and see how the magic is made. It is a consistent and reliable revenue generator. I had a vision to create a similar experience for visitors at The Studios.

## The Studio Tours

My first partner and I had a pleasant relationship, but he didn't share my vision for the public tour. So, after a year I asked my friend Ross Perot, Jr. if he would be willing to help me out and buy my partner's share of The Studios. He agreed, so we separated the tour out from the Studio soundstage operations, and I began creating a tour for the public that would give them that behind-the-scenes access I felt they might enjoy. The tour included several interactive shows demonstrating various aspects of the filmmaking process, a documentary on the early days of the film business, a special effects show, a "beam me up, Scotty" exhibit, a demonstration of blue-screen technology, and secrets of film makeup. And of course, they got to see the soundstages where many hit movies were made.

I also began buying all the recognizable movie memorabilia I could find. Among the items I collected was the original Frankenstein laboratory and a figure from the classic film *E. T. The Extraterrestrial*. This E.T. didn't have all the sophisticated animatronics, but it represented one of the great movies of all time, so it was very interesting to the public. I went to Los Angeles to pick it up. But then I faced a challenge—how would we get it home? It was huge, and E.T.'s arms were extended wide, like a basketball player defending the ball. In the end, I had to find a large plane and book an entire row of five seats in the middle of the cabin. What an odd sight it must have been for people at Los Angeles Airport to see me, several security people, and E.T. walking down the corridors together! It was an effort, but we got E.T. home.

Ultimately, The Studios had one of the largest collections of A-list movie memorabilia in the world. I acquired Dorothy's dress from *The Wizard of Oz*, the submarine from *The Hunt for Red October*, the guitars used in *Wayne's World*, the Batman suit Michael Keaton wore in the movie *Batman Returns*, the red space suit Robin Williams wore in the TV show *Mork and Mindy*, and a huge col-lection of *Star Trek* and *Star Wars* memorabilia. After Oliver Stone filmed his movie *JFK* at The Studios, he left the oval office replica there. And my favorite collection—the costumes from the classic family film *The Sound of Music*—ended up being the largest collection of its kind in the world. (When we made that collection public, Dan Truitt, who played Rolf in *The Sound of Music*, came to The Studios for the unveiling.)

## Eric Clapton

Almost every year, the singer and guitar legend Eric Clapton would spend two weeks at The Studios rehearsing for his national summer tour. Toward the end of his rehearsals, he'd always invite the studio employees to sit in Stage B and watch a full run-through of his show.

What a treat, to have Eric Clapton with his all-star band performing for our little group of employees!

On one of those occasions, Eric was rehearsing for the Crossroads Guitar Festival that was being held at Fair Park in Dallas. His band that year included Steve Gadd on drums, Nathan East on bass, Billy Preston on organ, Doyle Bramhall on slide guitar—and of course, Eric Clapton. The Crossroads Festival was filmed and released as a double DVD in 2004, which did extremely well. It's a real *who's who* of guitar players. That DVD includes bonus scenes of Eric driving up to The Studios in his cool hot rod and rehearsing there with his band.

 Whenever Eric came through The Studios, it gave me a chance to visit with my long-time friend Nathan East, who played bass for him. We had worked together on Christian albums countless times. And we would collaborate again when we co-wrote and co-produced for some major artists on a Christmas project for RadioShack in 2005.

Another fun time at the Studios was in 1992 when Phil Collins and Genesis filmed their video for the single *"Jesus He Knows Me"*. The video was entirely filmed at the Studios with Phil playing a televangelist. The video opened with Phil getting out of a limo in the Studios. The single from the album *We Can't Dance* went to number 12 on the

US Billboard Top 40 Mainstream chart and number 23 on the Top 100 chart.

In the video near the 1.40-minute mark people can be seen holding a sign reading "Genesis 3.25", not referring to the Bible but to the fact that the band had three members and had been together for twenty-five years. Some, not understanding this reference, believed the sign to be an error, as the third chapter in the Book of Genesis has only 24 verses. The video was nominated at the Brit Awards in the British Video category in 1993.

When the filming of the video was completed, Phil left his orange jacket with a G patch and his signature on the jacket for the Studio tour.

The Studio tour was very successful for years. Ross and I also purchased the remaining forty-two acres of land surrounding the complex, which we eventually sold to Fox Sports Southwest for their broadcast center as well as some other companies. It was a worthwhile endeavor—and lots of fun. But in my life there always seems to be a new adventure around the corner. After I received a phone call from Mark Hill at RadioShack, it looked like the time had come to sell The Studios at Las Colinas.

When I sold the Studios, I did not sell the movie memorabilia I had collected. Years later, I began to sell the items used in the movie studio tour and discovered that during the twenty years I'd owned them their value had risen quite a bit. In 2013 most of *The Sound of Music* costumes, my favorite collection, sold in a Profiles in History auction. It fetched an amazing price.

# 16

# Gerbert's World

Being a father of young children, I came to realize how important it is for kids to have positive instruction to deal with life's hard issues. Sesame Street did a great job of teaching reading, writing, and arithmetic. But what about daily life situations—such as a child whose parents are divorcing, or who has lost a family member to illness? These are real things that happen to kids. And they need help to understand how to cope with them. Some events are less tragic but can still have a big impact on impressionable young children—such as having a friend move away or seeing a neighbor suffering with special needs. I developed a real passion for developing a Christian-based program to address these issues.

I found a kindred spirit in Tim Robertson, the son of Pat Robertson, founder of the Christian Broadcasting Network. I had been a guest on CBN's *The 700 Club* many times and our families had gone skiing together, so I got to know Tim well. We were at a similar stage of life then, with preschool-aged children. And we both saw the urgent need for a children's program with a Christian emphasis.

Meanwhile, my brother Brad had become friends with Andy Holmes from Abilene, a puppeteer who was doing children's shows in churches around town. Andy had a little puppet character he called *Gerbert.* Brad and I approached him with the idea of developing Gerbert into a television show for preschoolers. It could be a wonderful vehicle for

presenting positive Christian values to a wide audience. Andy liked the idea, so we struck a deal. Then we presented the project to Tim Robertson at CBN. He liked it too and agreed to help.

In 1987, we taped the first thirteen episodes of the Gerbert TV series at the CBN studios in Virginia Beach, Virginia. Brad was responsible for the production through our company. I wrote and produced the music and sound effects and handled the business and distribution. Andy Holmes remained the voice and puppet master. The show began airing on CBN on February 15, 1988.

Since I was a father of preschoolers, the Gerbert series was dear to my heart. I'd bring home the rough edits as they became available and show them to my own kids. They were the perfect test group!

When I purchased The Studios at Las Colinas, we had a ready-made venue for producing Gerbert, so we taped the next twenty-six episodes there and I recorded the music at my home recording studio. Meanwhile, Brad had developed a friendship with Kermit Love, the puppeteer who worked with Jim Henson and developed many of the Muppets seen on Sesame Street. Brad had Kermit create an updated version of the Gerbert puppet using orange material that made it more lifelike and interesting.

We knew that preschoolers love music, so there was plenty of music in each Gerbert episode. We later compiled the music from each show and released sixteen audio projects. Word Music distributed the music to the Christian market along with videos of the TV shows. Those videos and cassettes were also sold in Walmart and other national retail outlets.

The Gerbert shows continued to appear on CBN and were later broadcast on PBS, ABC, The Family Channel, and other outlets. Gerbert became the number one children's character in the Christian market and was the "Mickey Mouse" of the Christian world for more than ten years. The series won the cable TV industry's Ace Award for Best Preschool Show, and the Gospel Music Association's Dove Award in the same category.

After fifty video episodes and sixteen audio projects, we felt we had produced enough. After all, the preschool audience changes every four years, so the show would still be a fresh experience for each generation of young viewers. And as my own kids moved out of the preschool phase my interest shifted too. My brother Brad went on to produce *Whirligig*, another children's program, with Kermit Love. Eventually the driving force behind Gerbert dissipated and *Veggie Tales* took its place as the top Christian children's TV series. But Gerbert is still shown around the world today.

One of the unique things about the series is that Gerbert is the only puppet in the show—all the other charac-ters are humans. Also, viewers hear—but never see—Gerbert's parents, so he has no race; he is just orange. That was intentional from the beginning. And I think the shows and its topics have held up well over the years. Young kids still need encouragement and instruction. And they still love adorable characters.

Before we began the Gerbert TV series, we produced a single video which was released on VHS. My brother Brad arranged to have it taped at a studio in Allen, Texas. It included a duet with me and my young daughter Courtney, singing *He's Got the Whole World in His Hands*. At the end of the song, Courtney spontaneously asked, "Daddy, How many hands does God have?" I'm sure that innocent ad lib melted a lot of hearts. We released the duet of Courtney and me to Christian radio and it reached the Top 10 in the CCM charts.

The studio where we recorded that video was owned by Richard Leach, the head of a large Catholic distribution company. After we produced it, I got a call from someone in Mr. Leach's office. He wanted to discuss another idea with me: a show for preschoolers that would star a purple dinosaur. "That's crazy," I told him. "That will never fly!"

Well. The first episode of *Barney & Friends* aired on April 6, 1992. And Barney the Dinosaur became the most popular preschool character in the world.

We began the Gerbert series with our own preschool children in mind. But now I'm a *grandfather* of preschoolers—and I find that they enjoy it too. I just might need to step into Gerbert's world one more time.

# 17

# A Dallas Cowboys Christmas

Being from Abilene, Texas, I was always a huge Dallas Cowboys fan. I inherited that from my Dad. We planned our week around the Cowboys games. When game day came, we turned on the TV and my dad would sit back in his leather chair wearing his goofy Dallas Cowboys fishing hat, with me on the floor beside him. I still have that  old hat in my office. It brings back a lot of great memories.

## Danny White and Tom Landry

My enthusiasm for the Cowboys endured, even after I had moved to Beverly Hills. I got to know Coach Tom Landry and then-quarterback Danny White when we worked together on numerous charity events in Dallas. So, when the Cowboys had their training camp in Thousand Oaks, California, Danny and I would sometimes get together during his time off.

Danny had always wanted to meet Cheryl Ladd, the actress and singer. He knew that I was friends with Cheryl and her husband Brian Russell. So one day I arranged for both Cheryl and Danny to come to my home. Cheryl was a big sports fan herself, so I think they were glad to meet each other.

Danny and I shared a strong commitment to our faith. He is also one of the calmest, most even-tempered guys I've ever known. Once he visited our home while Courtney, our first child, was less than a year old. We were enjoying a nice time together when Danny suddenly said, "Give me Courtney and I'll show you something." He took our little girl, put her small feet in the palm of his right hand and lifted her up almost to the ceiling. Her legs locked, and Danny balanced her there for what seemed like forever. As young first-time parents, we were mortified. But Danny had a house full of kids, so we figured he knew what he was doing.

In Dallas, I often visited Danny and his wife Jo Lynn at their home after a Cowboys game. Danny was always so cool and collected that I couldn't see any difference in him regardless of whether they'd just won or lost. That was Danny. Often, we went to dinner with our wives at Celebration Restaurant on Lovers Lane in Dallas. It was Danny's favorite place, with some great home cooking. We both loved chicken fried steak, mashed potatoes, gravy, homemade biscuits and green beans. So, one night at dinner, we were talking about our shared interests. Danny loved to sing and play the piano. And he really wanted to record an album. I told him I'd love to meet all the Dallas Cowboys. That's when we came up with the idea for a Dallas Cowboys Christmas album. We could record music and a video, involving the team and Coach Landry in the project, and donate the profits to Charity.

This was the year after the players of the Chicago Bears had a big hit with their recording of *The Super Bowl Shuffle*, so there was clearly an audience for such a project. We began lining up sponsors and went together to the headquarters of Minyard Food Stores, a popular grocery chain based in Dallas. There we met with Sonny Williams and Liz Minyard, who agreed to sponsor the project and have the album and video for sale at their store checkout stands. Liz was also on the board of the North Texas Food Bank and we agreed to give the profits to that organization. Meanwhile, Danny enlisted Coach Landry and the Cowboys players in the project while I began writing and producing the album. Some of the Players who participated were Danny White, Tony

Dorsett, Tony Hill, Mike Renfro, Doug Crosbie, Eugene Lockhart, Everson Walls, Ron Fellows, Dextor Clinkscale, Rafael Septien, Mike Saxon, Bill Bates—and, of course, Coach Landry.

One of the songs the Cowboys recorded for the first album was the well-known *Twelve Days of Christmas*. I wrote football verses and instead of "and a partridge in a pear tree", I changed the last line to "and a new hat for coach Landry." In the video, Tom puts on different hats for the first eleven verses and shakes his head and frowns. On the final verse, he puts on the correct hat—his trademark fedora—and smiles. It was really cute, and Tom was a great sport.

Danny White remembers another funny incident that happened with Tony Dorsett during the recording:

 When Tony was trying to record his vocal on one of the songs that had a certain rhythm and beat, he just could not get it right. He would come in wrong, get ahead of the beat, get behind the beat, he just couldn't nail it. After many attempts, he got frustrated, threw his headphones on the ground and went outside the studio to have a beer. When he came back in, Tony gave the same vocal another try. The same thing happened, he couldn't nail it. He once again threw his headphones on the ground and went out for another beer. This happened six to eight times, and when he came in the last time, something happened. He was relaxed and feeling it. Tony nailed it and we had ourselves a great performance.

*Dallas Cowboys Christmas* was released in the fall of 1985. The Cowboys had a winning season that year, so the album and video were a great success, bringing in close to $500,000. We were able to give a very nice check to the North Texas Food Bank.

With the success of that effort, we decided to do it again in 1986. I wrote some new songs and added some of my labels Christmas masters. Danny convinced many current Cowboys players to participate, including Herschel Walker, Brian Baldinger, Gordon Banks, Bill Bates, Tony Dorsett, Ron Fellows, Tony Hill, Jim Jeffcoat, Eugene Lockhart, Nate Newton, Steve Pelluer, Phil Pozderac, Mike Renfro, Mark Tuinei, Everson Walls, Danny White himself, Ed "Too Tall" Jones, and, again—Coach Landry.

I thought of a new idea for the '86 album. The Cowboys had a program that enabled them to involve alumni players in their community events, called *Dallas Cowboys Legends*. I thought this group could be a good addition to our production. "Why don't I write a song about the *good ole days*?" I said to Danny. "And maybe you could get some of the Cowboys Legends players to contribute on the new album." Danny started making phone calls. The response was wonderful. We recorded *Those Were the Good Old Days*, and made a video with the Cowboys Legends singing that included footage from many of the classic Cowboys games and training camps. Lee Martin helped us acquire the rights to use some great Cowboys legacy footage and did a great job producing the video. Some of the Legends who participated were Roger Staubach, Bob Breunig, Bob Hayes, Cliff Harris, Rayfield Wright, Preston Pearson—and, again, Tom Landry, wearing his signature hat as well as some sunglasses. These were probably the only times Tom Landry performed on a record and he was a great sport through the long days of taping.

Ch 17. A Dallas Cowboys Christmas

The album was released in October of 1986. Everything was moving along smoothly and successfully, just like the year before. Then on November 2, the Cowboys were playing the New York Giants when New York linebacker Carl Banks tackled Danny White. The fall broke Danny's wrist. With their starting quarterback sidelined, the Cowboys ended the second half of the season with just one win and seven losses. They did not make the playoffs. Unfortunately, sales of the album seemed to follow the win-loss record of the Cowboys. We were still able to write a nice check to the North Texas Food Bank, but not as big as the previous year. Both albums were fun projects for Danny and me. He got to sing and make his album. I got to meet all the Cowboys. And we all helped a worthwhile charity. Danny has been asked many times what some of his favorite memories are of being a Dallas Cowboy, and he doesn't hesitate: It was making the *Dallas Cowboys Christmas* albums—and helping a worthy cause.

## A Little Cowboy Diplomacy

In 1989, Dallas Cowboys owner Bum Bright sold the team to Jerry Jones. Shortly after that, Jones fired Tom Landry as coach, replacing him with Jimmy Johnson. Understandably, that led to some bruised feelings between the two coaches. During the time I owned The Studios at Las Colinas, Jimmy Johnson filmed a lot of commercials and charity videos there. And of course, I knew Tom Landry, so I had a relationship with both men. One day Jimmy's assistant came into my office. She told me that Jimmy planned to hold an event to benefit his charity, the Jimmy Johnson Foundation. They wanted to auction off a Dallas Cowboys helmet signed by Jimmy and Tom Landry as well as Roger Staubach, and Troy Aikman—the only two Cowboys coaches at that time, and the only Cowboys quarterbacks who had been Super

Bowl MVP's. And they wanted all four men to take a photo with the auction winner. Jimmy Johnson was aware that I knew Tom Landry, so he sent his assistant to ask me to present the idea to Tom and see if he would participate.

This was a delicate matter, but Jimmy was a good client of the Studios and Tom was a friend. So, I felt I should at least meet with Tom and ask. I said, "I'll talk to Tom. I don't know what he'll say, but I'll ask him."

I called Tom and asked if I could come visit; there was something I needed to ask him. A few days later, I was sitting with Tom Landry in his office in Dallas at Preston Center. Tom and I had a shared faith and similar values, so we spent ten minutes talking about those things and our families. Then, I took a deep breath and explained why I was there. "I know this is a touchy situation," I said, "But I told Jimmy I would at least ask".

Tom shifted in his chair, looked up for a few seconds, and finally replied, "Tell Jimmy I will accept his invitation on one condition. There must be *two* helmets, signed by all four of us, auctioned off to two people for the same amount for each helmet. And we all take a picture with the two winning bidders. All the proceeds from one helmet will go to my charity, Fellowship of Christian Athletes. And the proceeds from the other helmet can go to Jimmy's charity."

I was pleased to let Jimmy know that Tom had agreed to show up at his auction. But I knew it was only to help the Fellowship of Christian Athletes. That was who Tom was—someone who would put his own feelings and pride aside to help others.

When the auction was held, I stayed in the bidding to make sure it went as high as possible. And the helmets fetched $25,000 each. When it was all over, I was one of the winning bids and had my picture taken with Troy Aikman, Roger Staubach, Tom Landry, and Jimmy Johnson. And I left with an autographed Cowboys helmet.

To my knowledge, that was the only time Tom Landry and Jimmy Johnson spoke, or were even in the same room together, before Tom passed away in 2000. I know for sure that there are only two Dallas Cowboys helmets with those four signatures. Tom was a classy guy who walked his talk. I later recorded a tribute to Tom Landry with Gerry Beckley singing the backgrounds called "Man Behind the Man". I included Tom speaking at the end of the song.

*Tom Landry*

December 23, 1988

Mr. Chris Christian
P.O. Box 7409
Dallas, Texas 75209

Dear Chris:

Just a note to thank you for your thoughtfulness in remembering me at Christmas time with one of your tapes. I will really enjoy listening to it this Holiday Season.

I also appreciate your words of support. This has been one of the toughest seasons I can remember; however, I do feel we have built a good foundation for our future. We'll be back on top again soon.

Again, thanks for sharing your music with me. My best to you and your family for a blessed Christmas and a great 1989.

Sincerely yours,

*Tom Landry*

Tom Landry

TL:bg

COWBOYS CENTER ★ ONE COWBOYS PARKWAY ★ IRVING, TEXAS 75063-4727 ★ 214-556-9900

FOUNDATION FOR
CHILDREN'S CHARITIES

May 13, 1993

Mr. Chris Christian
President & CEO
Studios of Las Colinas
6301 North O'Connor Boulevard
Irving, Texas 75039

Dear Chris:

Thank you for your support and participation with my first fund raiser for the Jimmy Johnson Foundation for Children's Charities. I truly appreciate your efforts in helping to make this a successful event. It was the individual effort by each and every one of you that came together to make this a first-class weekend.

Since that time, the Dallas Cowboys have reported to camp looking like they are ready to work. I know that my efforts now will stay focused on football, but I will not forget that it was because of yours and many others like you who made it possible for us to generate some revenue to help kids in our community.

We can all be proud when we look to the end zone of Texas Stadium at a Cowboys home game and see hundreds of smiling faces of kids who received a free ticket as a reward to attend a Cowboys game because they worked hard to improve their grades and had good attendance records. Thank you for helping me to set a good example for our youth.

Sincerely yours,

*Jimmy*

Jimmy Johnson

JJ:bg *Chris - sorry our other deal did not work - appreciate your help!*

Little did I know I was about to be given an opportunity from a retail store that would be my biggest opportunity yet.

# 18

# RadioShack Days

It was 2003 when I got a call from Mark Hill, the senior vice president and general counsel of RadioShack. He told me the president of RadioShack, David Edmondson, had a proposal for me to consider and wanted to invite me to a secret dinner so we could discuss it. We agreed to meet at a restaurant in Irving, just outside of Dallas. When the day came, I drove to Cool River Café, just a stone's-throw from The Studios. As I walked through the big natural wood doors, I still had no idea what I was about to get into. I went inside where Dave and Mark greeted me. Before we got down to business, Mark presented me with a nondisclosure and confidential agreement to sign. This was all still very mysterious, but I was all ears. He went on to explain his idea, and it was a big one.

## A Vertically-Integrated Media Company

Dave's vision was to change RadioShack from a company that sold batteries, connectors, and gadgets to a content company. To do that, he intended to leverage all of RadioShack's existing relationships with Dish Network, Sirius Satellite Radio, Hewlett Packard, and Motorola. The company would create content—music in particular—which it would own. It would then distribute and sell that content through its partners' existing media channels, and RadioShack retail outlets. This new company would have its own national radio outlet through Sirius, its own TV music channel through DISH Network, its content embedded on Motorola cell phones, and its own app on the desktops of HP computers. Meanwhile, all 6,000 RadioShack retail outlets would have the CDs for sale at the cash registers and marketing loops of the content playing on the store TVs. David didn't realize it at the time, but I said "David, what you have outlined to me is a vertically-integrated media company—something that, up until now, has never existed."

But that was just the beginning. Dave also wanted to create a system for nurturing and developing aspiring music artists, like the farm system that exists in baseball. In baseball you go from Pee Wee League, Little League, Colt League, and on through the Minor Leagues. Then if you're good enough, you could reach the Major Leagues and enjoy national success. At that time, no such path existed for artists. And it still doesn't. I knew enough about the mindset of young musicians to realize this would be a very appealing idea for them. David sketched out a diagram of his vision, with lots of interlocking circles, showing how each company would contribute to the plan, creating synergy. In discussions after that, I fondly referred to Dave's diagram as *Tiny Bubbles.*

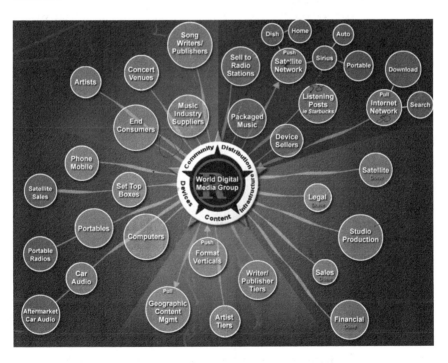

I was blown away by his two ideas. Simply put, there was no record company on earth with its own national radio station, TV channel, and 6,000 retail outlets to market and sell its product. Music could be sold physically in stores, and digitally on cell phones—which RadioShack sold as well. At the time, RadioShack was the largest seller of cell phones to women in the country. I saw the possibilities immediately. So, I came onboard as a consultant and the leader of a discovery group whose mission was to explore the viability of the project. I reported directly to Mark Hill. The discovery group consisted of representatives picked by the CEO of each prospective company. With so many Fortune 500 companies involved, it was very important to keep the project's existence and activities confidential. So, the group had a code name: Elvis.

By this time, the coffee chain Starbucks was selling music CDs at its retail locations, a first-of-its-kind innovation. Dave and I speculated that Starbucks might want to join our venture. If they did, that would add more than 10,000 retail outlets to the mix. So, RadioShack's CEO and president, along with Mark Hill and I, got in the RadioShack plane and flew to Seattle. There we presented the idea to Starbucks CEO Howard Schultz and the Starbucks entertainment team. Before the meeting began, Howard showed us some clips from the Ray Charles movie, *Genius Loves Company*, which they were about to release.

In the end, the two companies didn't end up joining forces. But that was an interesting meeting, to say the least. And Howard Schultz was kind enough to give me a black Starbucks apron to take home.

After working secretly for a year-and-a-half, our discovery group was ready to make its presentation to the prospective RadioShack partners. We met at the Gaylord Hotel in Grapevine Texas in May 2004, with representatives from RadioShack, DISH Network, Sirius Satellite Radio, Hewlett Packard, Billboard Live, Motorola and Media Net—and me. Dave Edmondson stood up before this roomful of presidents, CEOs and other top executives and he gave his pitch. Then the representatives from each company expressed their particular views, and I closed with a financial projection of what this company could be worth in five years. At the end, David stood up, looked around at everyone, and asked, "Who's in?"

*Everyone* was in.

As it turned out, Hewlett Packard had some stipulations that Dave found unworkable, so the project moved ahead without them. But *World Digital Media Group* (WDMG) was launched in May 2005, as a collaboration between RadioShack, DISH Network and Sirius Satellite Radio. I was CEO.

This had to be the greatest opportunity to come my way since, well, the Elvis days. I knew I wouldn't be able to launch WDMG and run The Studios at Las Colinas at the same time. So, I sold The Studios and completely dove into my new venture.

With the huge platform that WDMG offered, I had a compelling proposal to offer major music artists. I asked Nathan East, my old friend in L.A., to help me reach some of them. Nathan was close with almost every major artist, and he gave me the opportunity to work with many of them. Together, he and I wrote and produced music for Natalie Cole, Patti Austin, Al Jarreau, the Pointer Sisters, Ali Lohan, Fourplay, and Kirk Whalum.

We wanted to make the company's first releases available for Christmas, which meant delivering the finished product to RadioShack by October. That gave us just four months to complete the first batch of CDs. But somehow, we did it. Nathan proved to be an invaluable help, pulling together all the artists and making it happen on schedule. By November we had recorded, purchased, or leased many recordings and released them through RadioShack. In addition to the artists above, we purchased or acquired the rights for CDs by Willie Nelson, Waylon Jennings, Vanessa Williams, Jim Brickman, All-4-One, David Pack, John Tesh, Michael W. Smith and Amy Grant. We also filmed 505 high-definition videos of songs by the top independent bands in the country. These would appear on the flagship show on YMC.TV, our channel on DISH Network. It was quite a whirlwind of productive activity and the future for WDMG looked limitless. But as quickly as it started, it came to an abrupt end.

## The End of the Vision

David Edmondson was forced out as President of RadioShack. And his successor didn't share his vision. Less than two years after we had begun, the new president of RadioShack had his attorneys contact me. They wanted out. I invited them to come visit with me to get a better understanding of what WDMG was. I really believed we'd had a successful start and there was great potential for growth. But their message was clear and unbending—*they wanted out*. For the first time I was learning how Fortune 500 companies think. And the lesson was not a happy one. David and Mark knew that RadioShack could not survive with its existing business model. They had a vision to transform it into a content, marketing and media company. And by leveraging its strong current relationships, the company was poised to change the music industry on a scale never seen before. But now, just like that, it was all gone.

I arranged for the purchase of the WDMG assets. RadioShack declared Chapter 11 bankruptcy in 2015, and again in 2017. At this writing there are fewer than 600 RadioShack stores remaining.

Looks like Mark and David might have been right.

# 19

# Basketball

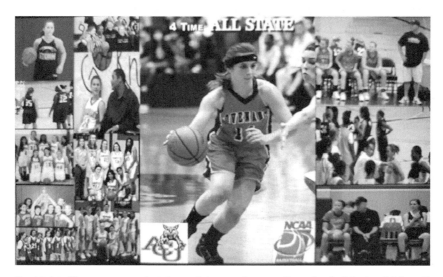

In 1992 Shanon gave birth to Savannah, our fourth child. And like all kids, Savannah turned out to be full of surprises. She had many talents, but as she grew it became obvious that she excelled at one thing in a spectacular way—sports. Especially, basketball. Her grandfather had played for Abilene Christian and I played through high school. But Savannah took the game to a whole new level. In elementary and junior high school she was always the best at any sport she tried. Then, in high

school she began serious basketball training and became a four-time All-State basketball player in Texas to add to her five state track championship metals.

## That World-Famous Game

Savannah also participated in one of the most famous—or, infamous—high school basketball games in history. Her school, Dallas Covenant, was playing Dallas Academy. And Savannah's team won by an unlikely score of 100 to 0. (This was the second game Savannah had scored 48 points.) The game ended like every other game, with high-fives all around. But the rout was so unusual that it merited a front-page story in the Dallas Morning News. The story was then picked up by national media, and ultimately went around the world. There was a story in Sports Illustrated. It was mentioned in blogs and in the pre-game TV coverage of that year's Super Bowl. ESPN's show *Outside the Lines* came to Dallas to interview Savannah's coach Micah Grimes. There was also much discussion on the ESPN show, *Pardon the Interruption*. The game was even mentioned in one of Jay Leno's monologues on *The Tonight Show*.

It should have been an inspiring story of how hard work and dedication can lead to success. But instead, it ignited a nationwide controversy. Some people said it was harmful for the losing team to suffer such a humiliating defeat. Others pointed out that such a terrible loss might spur them to work harder. But the media ran with the Dallas News version, which was based on one interview with one mom from the losing side. And many of the important facts were never reported.

For instance, by halftime it was clear the score was going to be very one-sided, so Coach Grimes asked the opposing coach if he wanted to stop the game. But that coach felt it would be too humiliating for his girls. He said, "Play on." For the rest of the game, Grimes had Savannah's team go for three-point shots—the hardest to make—just to slow down the scoring. Some reports also noted that Savannah's team only used their starters. The implication was that they were so obsessed with winning that they cast aside the common high school practice of letting everyone play. But Savannah's team only had seven players, three of whom planned to play college basketball. There was no "bench" to bring in!

Political correctness quickly took over and ran amok. The incredible result was that the girls who had trained year-round to perfect their craft were criticized. And Micah Grimes, the coach who had led his team from a losing record the previous year to great success, was fired. I felt bad for him. I happened to film that game, so I had lots of opportunity to ponder what went on. It showed me how a media frenzy can quickly distort the facts--and how important it is to respond to misinformation by getting the real story out as fast as possible.

## Savannah's Great Career

The national attention was painful for Savannah, but she kept doing what she loved and practicing to perfect her basketball skills. Later, she had the opportunity to play for Team Texas, one of the best AAU teams in the state, and the Elite California Storm, one of the top Nike teams in the nation.

There was nothing I loved more than traveling with Savannah to basketball tournaments around the country and watching her play. It gave me lots of opportunities to use my creativity. I filmed all her games and training sessions from the third grade to her University NCAA tournament. *(Would that qualify for an over the top proud dad?)* Each film would include an opening, dissolves, credits, and music, as if it were a major motion picture. Sometimes I got so consumed with the film process, zoom-ins and -outs, camera angles, and B-roll footage that I wouldn't really see the game until I got home and watched what I'd filmed. Savannah, of course, thought I was *nuts*. After all, she didn't see any other parents filming their kids' games. But she didn't realize that I just loved seeing her play—and that making a movie of every game offered me a creative outlet. It was all worth it when at the end of her career I asked her what her greatest memory was of her wonderful basketball career. She said, "It was spending time with you, Dad".

## Dan Cathy

While I was in Atlanta for one of Savannah's tournaments, I decided to call my long-time friend Dan Cathy, the head of Chick-fil-A. I asked if he'd like to get together. "I've got to work the phones on Friday," he said, "but I'd love for you to come out and sit with me. We can visit in between calls."

I wasn't sure what he meant, but I said, "Sure. I'll be there." As I entered the Chick-fil-A campus and drove up the long, winding road lined with beautiful pines, I marveled at the phenomenal success the company had enjoyed. And I was eager to catch up with my old friend. In the lobby, Dan's assistant came down to meet me and then took me on a tour. She showed me the cool car collection that Truett Cathy, the company's founder, had assembled. It included the Batmobile from the TV series *Batman*. Then she took me down to the basement where they test all their new food offerings. I got to sample some of the things that would be showing up in their stores in the future. There was history all over the walls, and even a museum area that told the story of Chick-fil-A—how Truett Cathy had begun a little restaurant called the Dwarf House, and that evolved into one of the most popular food chains in the country. Afterward I was ushered into the phone room, where the company received calls from any unsatisfied customers.

And there sitting by the phone was Dan Cathy, the head of Chick-fil-A.

"What do you do here?" I asked him.

Dan said, "Our top executives take one shift each week to listen to customer complaints, try to resolve their issues, and make them happy. We never want to lose touch with our customers, and having our top executives listen to them directly helps us stay close to them." I thought, *Wow, I wonder how many companies do that?* Anyone wondering about how Chick-fil-A achieved its success need look no further than that phone room—and the amazing dedication to customer service that Dan Cathy and Chick-fil-A exemplifies.

Fortunately for me, this was a very slow complaint day, so Dan and I enjoyed a wonderful visit in the phone room that continued as he walked me to his office. (I'll never forget all the cows hanging on the walls. They were everywhere!) As we continued to chat I discovered we had something in common besides our commitment to faith and family. It was a love for John Deere tractors. I left Dan's office with a new appreciation for my friend—and a signed copy of Truett Cathy's book, which I cherish to this day.

## Choosing a College

Savannah's achievements on the court were matched by a stellar academic record, so she was recruited by many Division 1 Universities, including Harvard, Princeton, Dartmouth, Georgetown and Rice. We began hitting the road on father-daughter trips, visiting the colleges she had received letters from. That enabled us to get to know the people and campuses behind the letters. When we went to New Hampshire to visit Dartmouth, the weather was rainy and cold. That didn't suit Savannah, who was raised on the sunny plains of Texas. She wasn't shy about making her preferences known. "Dad," she said, "I'm not going to attend here. Can we go on to Harvard?"

"No," I said, "we have dinner tonight with the coach!" But I had to laugh to myself.

We did go to Harvard, and Princeton, and Times Square for fun. Of course, I had a video running most of the time. But we both knew she didn't want to move to the Northeast to play basketball.

We also went to Aspen for a meeting of owners of professional sports teams. There, Savannah and I met Jerry Colangelo, president of USA Basketball who presented her with a once-in-a-lifetime opportunity. He invited her to work for USA basketball at the upcoming 2012 Olympics in London. Savannah thoroughly enjoyed that experience, and I'll always be grateful to Jerry for providing it.

Rice University in Houston seemed like a good prospect for Savannah. It was well-regarded academically, and was relatively close to our home in Dallas, so it wouldn't be too hard for us to attend all her games. I knew the school's great reputation but wasn't familiar with its basketball program. I called Paul Hobby, a friend in Houston, and asked if he had any contacts there who knew about basketball at Rice. He arranged a meeting for me with a man named Bobby Tudor.

We flew down to Houston on Southwest Airlines. There, we met with Greg Williamson, the school's head basketball coach, and Chris Del-Conte, the athletic director. After a while I left Savannah to continue talking with them and walked over to the campus café to meet Bobby Tudor. I introduced myself and settled in for a conversation. He was extremely enthusiastic about the program and obviously very knowledgeable. After a few minutes I asked him, "Why are you so passionate—and so knowledgeable—about Rice and its basketball program?"

"I played basketball here," Bobby explained, "and, I'm the chairman of the board. I walked away thinking, *Well, my friend Paul really came through!* As I returned to the steps of the Rice gym I glanced up to see the inscription on the front of the building. It read, *Tudor Field House*. So, I had obviously been talking to the right man.

Eventually, Savannah decided to carry on the family legacy and attend Abilene Christian University. After all, her great-grandfather had been vice president, her grandfather played basketball there, and it was my alma mater as well. It was a terrific choice and Savannah definitely thrived. In her junior year, her team won the Lone Star Conference Championship. She asked me if I'd mind if she ended her basketball career after that. She just wanted to enjoy a normal senior year of college.

## Another Opportunity

It was a great ending to a great basketball career for Savannah. But along the way, as usual, some unexpected opportunities dropped into my lap. When I was meeting with Greg Williamson the basketball coach at Rice, he mentioned that Donna Orender, the President of the Women's National Basketball Association, would like to speak with me. I called her from the Rice campus and she asked if I'd be interested in buying the local WNBA team, the Houston Comets. Donna also invited me to the WNBA semi-finals which were being held in Indianapolis that year. Of course, I accepted, and when the day came, off I flew to Indiana.

There was a pre-game reception where I struck up a conversation with a fellow from Oklahoma named Bill Cameron. I discovered that Bill and I shared a lot in common—both of us had daughters who were outstanding basketball players, and we were both members of the Young Presidents Organization (YPO). And, it turned out that both of us had also been approached about buying the Houston Comets. Neither one of us wanted to make a lot of trips to Houston. But I told him if there was ever a team in Dallas, I'd be interested in that. Bill was already an owner of an NBA team and he was in the process of moving the Detroit Shock, a WNBA team, to Tulsa, Oklahoma. So, he wondered if I might be interested in joining the ownership group there. "You can sit in the back seat as a minority owner," he said, "and then, if you ever have a chance to be involved in Dallas, you'll already have some experience."

It was a good point. "It sounds interesting," I said. But I didn't go any farther than that.

The next day, Bill called to see if I was interested. And I had been mulling over the idea since we spoke. Attending my daughter's games had brought me such joy, I thought it might be nice to have a team to follow when her career was over. And after twenty-five years in the entertainment business, it could be a fun diversion. So I agreed.

In 2009 I purchased a small share in what would become the Tulsa Shock. I was the only owner who didn't live in Oklahoma, but over the next six years I logged thousands of miles driving there and back. During that first year as a team owner, I was surprised to learn that professional sports is very similar to the entertainment business I had been in my whole life. Both are in the business of making stars, selling tickets to arena events, developing a supportive fan base, selling merchandise, and creating entertaining events. And at their best, both do good things for their communities. When I met with the other owners and found out how things were done, I said, "Well, this sounds like a band on tour. I understand that!"

After joining the Tulsa franchise, I immediately started talking to friends and owners of companies in Dallas to gauge what interest, if any, there might be in bringing a WNBA team to Dallas. A few years later, I talked to NBA commissioner Adam Silver in Aspen and presented my plan. He was positive on the idea of having a team in Dallas, but made it clear he couldn't give me a time frame for when the league might expand. I also talked to Mark Cuban—partly to make sure he wasn't planning to bring a WNBA team to Dallas himself. If he did want to, there'd be no need for me to keep laying the groundwork.

Mark was very courteous and said, "I've got my hands full with the Mavericks, and I don't think I have an interest, but if I can help you in any way please let me know."

So, with a clear runway, I began approaching potential stakeholders to discuss the possibility of bringing a team to Dallas. I met with prospective owners, university representatives, and owners of other venues that might have an interest. Donna Orender also flew down a couple of times to explain the league to those who were interested. Over a few years, we developed several potential sponsors, owners, and arena options.

While we were waiting for the league to expand, Bill Cameron called me with an unexpected proposal: What would I think about combining all the groundwork I'd already done in Dallas, and moving the Tulsa Shock to Dallas?

It was an interesting idea. I drove to Oklahoma to discuss it with him. On September 13, 2014, Bill and I met during halftime at an Oklahoma University home football game and came up with an agreement. Once we decided to move forward, I began meeting with the owners and sponsors I'd been talking with over the previous years to let them know there might be a real possibility—if we could get the league's approval. The Dallas group met the requirements and eventually the league approved. Now, the hard work of naming the team, picking the uniforms, designing the logo and colors, finding the right staff, selling tickets, getting sponsors, and finalizing the arena deal lay ahead. The Dallas Wings played their first game on May 28th, 2016 at UTA College Park Center.

# 20

# Music Babies

I've often compared writing a song to giving birth. One day a song doesn't exist and the next day, there it is. A music baby begins when an idea is conceived in a songwriter's imagination. The writer nourishes it, helps it develop, and finally brings it into the world. And like a new mother, every songwriter believes his or her music baby is beautiful. That writer doesn't know what will happen to that baby, where it will go or who it will touch. The songwriter hopes everyone will like their music baby but knows that not everyone will.

If I'm that songwriter, I'm going to make sure my music baby is presented as well as possible, by making a demo of the song. I'm going to introduce it to as many people as possible to help it succeed. At some point I'll even give it wings and send it out into the world. I know some will think it is beautiful, others won't. And some people will never see or hear it. (That's an analogy that might be helpful for every songwriter to remember.)

In my role as a producer I've watched some awesome music babies come into the world. And as a songwriter, I've given birth to some myself. Here are a few of the most memorable ones.

# Safe

One of the truly great singers I've had the opportunity to work with is Steve Archer. During Steve's long career, many of his best songs were penned by a songwriter named Jeremy Dalton. They included *Through His Eyes of Love*, which became Steve's first number one song—and the title of his first number one album.

Steve introduced me to him, and after hearing some of his songs I signed him to a publishing agreement. While we were selecting songs for Steve's next album *Action*, we listened to several tunes Jeremy had written. One called *Safe* really caught my ear. As I heard its great melody and the message that we are *safe inside God's love*, I knew it could be a number one hit. And if we could find a well-known artist to sing it as a duet with Steve, that would help get the record noticed. That's when I called Marilyn McCoo, whom I'd met years earlier when she was hosting the TV show *Solid Gold*. "Marilyn," I said, "How would you like to do a duet with Steve Archer?" I knew Marilyn was a Christian, but she had never done a Christian album. I was convinced that pairing these two extraordinary voices would yield a great result.

Marilyn agreed, so I began assembling some of the best musicians in L.A. for the recording. Our engineer was Jack Puig, who would later work with such artists as Supertramp and John Mayer. I brought in the A Team of musicians—Paul Leim, Abe Laboriel, Robbie Buchanan, and Dann Huff. With a team like that and a great song, we had our best chance for a hit. I was not surprised when *Safe* reached number one on the national Christian charts and was named one of the best records of the 80's.

## If You Were the Only One

Steve followed the success of *Safe* with a song I had in our publishing company and had been saving for the right artist and the right time. *If You Were the Only One* was written by Robert Sterling, Cindy Sterling, and Gary Floyd. It became the first single off Steve's 1988 album *Off the Page*. I added a fade vamp at the end of the song where Tim and Janice Archer added their sibling harmonies. They did an amazing job, as did Steve. Having all the Archers singing together made that music baby! That was a special record for me personally, as I played all the instruments except the Saxophone. That was possible because of the Linn 9000 drum machine sequencer. Once again, learning to play all those instruments during the Wayne Newton days paid off. This was the writers' song baby, but it was my *record* baby. And of course, I thought it was beautiful. It rose on the charts to number one and remains one of my favorite records. I still listen to it today.

## Walking Away With You

Amy Grant's career was going stronger than ever. Brown Bannister was officially handling her production by now, but I was still involved. We needed to find some songs for her *Never Alone* album and most of us were hoping to see her move in a more contemporary direction. The West Coast sound of Michael McDonald and Christopher Cross was very popular then. So, I co-wrote several songs in that vein with Amy, Brown, and Gary Chapman, including *Too Late, So Glad, It's a Miracle*, and my favorite—*Walking Away With You*. In my view, that song struck a perfect balance between who Amy was as an artist and what was happening in music at the time. The record and the video became some of Amy's most popular work of that time.

## Telephone Lines

In those days I often visited my buddy Steve Kipner at his home studio in Malibu, and almost every time we got together we'd end up writing some songs. We were both pretty fast writers, and one day he came up with a lyric idea: "I've had enough of your *telephone lines*." The word *lines* had a double meaning, referring to both a physical telephone line and the false lines a cheating lover might say over the phone. We fired up Steve's drum machine and soon had a demo of *Telephone Lines*, which was later recorded by Sheena Easton and included on her gold al-

bum "You Could Have Been With Me". Many of Steve's demos were so good that they became the track for some very well-known songs, such as *Genie in a Bottle*.

## Love's Not One to Forget

Kerry Chater was another writing partner I really enjoyed. He had been a member of the popular group Gary Puckett and the Union Gap. We didn't write a lot of songs together, but those we did are still among my favorites. One song, *Love's Not One to Forget*, was included on my pop album. Bob Gaudio made some additional changes that helped give the song its smooth, seamless quality. The result was a complicated arrangement that sounds deceptively simple.

## (Want You) Back in My Life Again

Neither Kerry nor I were thinking of the Carpenters when we wrote *(Want You) Back In My Life Again*. We thought it might be a song for my next album. But the Carpenters—my favorite group—recorded it and released it as a single. Through a strange set of circumstances, it was on the Billboard charts at the same time as my single, *I Want You, I Need You*. It was so fun to have two of my music babies on the charts at the same time.

## Light at the End of the Darkness.

I've always admired Larry Gatlin's songs, but there was one I especially loved: *Light at the End of the Darkness*. I decided to record it for my album *Just Sit Back*, and I asked Larry if he would sing on it too. He accepted. Larry arrived at Gold Mine for the recording. "Play me the track and your vocal and let me see what I can add," he said. Now remember, this was his music baby. When he heard me sing the final line at the end, he started screaming, "Christian, what are you doing to my song?"

I said "Larry, what's the problem?"

"You blew the last line!" he yelled. "It's not 'I was looking up FROM the bottom.' It's 'I was looking up THROUGH the bottom!'"

He was right; I had messed up his music baby. I stopped everything, went behind the microphone, and corrected the last line. After that, Larry was happy. He went on to overdub several harmony parts, using that famous high falsetto of his. I think those parts make the record. *Light at the End of the Darkness*

Ch 20. Music Babies

is one of my favorites of all the songs I recorded in Nashville. Lesson learned: Don't mess up someone else's music, baby!

## Forever Love

I was receiving about 100 cassettes a week from songwriters around the country, sending me their music babies. I didn't have time to listen to them during the week, so I had my assistant, Dawn Allen, put them all in a bag and give them to me when I traveled to concerts on weekends. On one trip, after landing at the airport I had to drive more than two hours to the concert. It was a beautiful day, so I rented a convertible with a cassette player. With my bag of demos open on the passenger side, I drove down a deserted country highway, putting tapes in and listening as I went. (I always listened to every cassette I received, because I knew sometimes I'd find a gem. I could usually tell after the first fifteen seconds whether it was worth listening to the whole tape.)

Left Photo: Dawn Allen. Right Photo: Eric Champion

This day, for some reason I began throwing the bad tapes out of the convertible as I drove. Then, about halfway to my destination, I put in a tape labeled "Eric Champion-Win." From the downbeat of the first song I knew there was something special about this artist. His music had the flavor of many Christian pop artists, but with a Michael Jackson/ Kenny Loggins/Prince/Stevie Wonder vocal approach. The rhythmic foundation had a Latin, futuristic, techno dance sound. He also had a unique way of presenting a ballad. Sure enough, the whole tape had a very different sound and style.

One song on that tape really impressed me, called *Forever Love*. When I got back home I called Eric and signed him to my production and publishing company. After that I stayed closely involved with his records and mixed all his albums. That song became Eric's first number one hit and was one of the Top 50 songs on the CCM charts for all of 1990. Eric had eight number one records on Christian radio and many other Top 40 hits in between.

I've always felt bad about littering the highway with all those cassette tapes and wondered if someone found one of those music babies and liked it. But Eric Champion's genius is a good example of why I listened to every tape I received.

## Day Like Today

I was in the middle of recording my album *Higher Ways*, and I needed some better songs than I had. I called Jeremy Dalton, who is one of the best songwriters I know, and asked if he could come to Dallas and help me out. He flew out with his wife Brenda and soon we were sitting together in my Dallas studio. Jeremy was at the grand piano playing some of his new songs. But I wasn't hearing anything that was right for me. After a while he said, "That's all the new songs I have."

Then Brenda said, "Play him that chorus I love. I can't remember the name …"

Jeremy objected. "That one's not finished," he said, "and anyway, I don't think it's that good."

He played it anyway. As I heard it I yelled, "You're crazy! That is a number one hit. And what a message!" We spent the rest of the day finishing *Day Like Today*. It had a background vocal part that was crucially important to the song and needed someone special to sing it. So, I called Gerry Beckley, my friend from the group America. He came to my studio in Dallas and—in between tennis games at the country club—we recorded his background harmonies. They had that very identifiable "America" sound. And sure enough, that song became my next number one Christian record. I performed it in the movie *Dakota* and consider it one of the greatest messages I've ever recorded. It would have not been the same record without Gerry!

## Not by Might, Not by Power

We had success taking the Imperials quartet in a more contemporary direction with *Sail On* and *Heed The Call*. Not to miss out on a possible trend, Bill Gaither had noticed this and formed a quartet. He asked if I could take his quartet in a contemporary direction like I had done with the Imperials. Bill and Gloria Gaither and I wrote a song we thought would be good for this album, *Not by Might, Not by Power*.

On the day we were to record the basic track, Bill had brought his father to the session at Gold Mine. Of all days, this day the drummer came in with his girlfriend, having stayed up all night, doing who

knows what. As he walked in late, or, should I say, stumbled in, Bill looked at me and said, "I don't think the drummer is going to be able keep time or be on the session. Chris, do you know how to play drums? And what a day to bring my father!"

I said I had practiced on some rubber drum practice pads at the Sands hotel when I worked for Wayne Newton, but I had never played drums live or on a session. Bill said, "Perfect! You're the drummer today." Fortunately, the song had a straight ahead 2/4-time signature. So, there I was in the drum booth at Gold Mine playing drums for the first time, and Brown took over the producing chores in the control room with

Bill. That was the first and the last time I ever played real drums on a session, but when drum sequencers were invented, I programmed the drums on almost every album.

Bill had not yet decided on the final name of the group, and the Starlight Vocal Band had a hit *Afternoon Delight* at that time. I said, "Why don't you call the group the *New Gaither Vocal Band*. So, the album had one track with a first-time drummer and the group had a name.

## Mark Heard Songs

With almost every music baby I produced or was involved with, I worked with the songwriter to push them to make their song the best it could be, at least from my viewpoint. Sometimes this was a lyric change, adding a fade ending, eliminating where a song would bog down, and other small changes that could make a song better. Most of the mothers of these music babies were very open to any suggestion that might make their song better, but there were a few that were not interested.

The only writer I ever signed and did not offer my opinions to was Mark Heard from Macon, Georgia. Simply because Mark had a vision for his music babies, and that was it.

Mark was a very "Bob Dylan" type songwriter and had traveled to Switzerland to study at L'Abri under the influential evangelical Christian philosopher Francis Schaefer.

Mark wrote biblical oriented songs but did not want to be known as a Christian songwriter and was a protégée of Christian rocker Larry Norman. Larry and Randy Stonehill discovered Mark Heard while hearing a tape of Mark singing some of his songs with just a guitar. Mark recorded an album for Larry's Solid Rock Records called Appalachian Melody. I had heard Larry was not going to continue to give Mark a platform to record so I reached out to meet Mark.

Mark was a unique songwriter who wrote very thoughtful lyrics. Sometimes he used a critical, "protest" type approach to get his message across. But something about his lyrics and style appealed to me. Up till then, I had always tried to make commercial records that reached a large audience, which wasn't Mark's main goal. He wanted to be free to express what he wanted to say the way he wanted to say it. I had enjoyed so much commercial success with Christian records; now I wanted to support Mark and give him a platform for his brilliant music and lyrics. So I signed him to a long-term record and publishing agreement.

No other label would sign him, but I wanted to help him get his music babies out into the world. I told him if he would sign with my label I'd let him have complete control over the songs, the music, the studio, the budget, and the artwork for each album he delivered under our agreement; I would simply provide the funds. This appealed to him, and after five albums he delivered to Home Sweet Home Records, we both did what we had agreed to do. Mark delivered the albums with covers he designed, and I paid for them and stayed completely out of his way. I never told him what songs he should record and I was never at one of his recording sessions.

I would usually hear the album when he delivered it to me and see the cover when he showed it to me. This was not at all how I usually worked with other artists but in Mark's case, I just wanted him to be Mark. I felt my commercial, pop, influence would be harmful for his

A Grandmother's Prayer

albums. And anyway, Mark wanted total control. I feel some of Mark Heard's songs and music have stood the test of time and are among the best original music babies ever released on Home Sweet Home Records.

Mark was generally angry at "The Man" and "The Establishment" and maybe some of that ended up being directed at me. But I always felt I gave him a chance to send his music babies into the world with no influence from me or anyone else—just what he wanted.

It was not Mark's style to say a traditional *thank you*, but I think a letter he sent me one day from Switzerland on his letterhead sums it up: "Officially, Thanks." Signed, *"Mark."* (See page 235 in the Appendix.)

## White Heart

Not all music babies have an easy time finding their place in the world. One of the demo tapes I received in those early days was from a group called White Heart. They approached every Christian music label they could find—and were turned down by them all. When I heard the demo of what would become their first album, I was totally blown away by their unique, powerful sound and great lyrics. They had a dynamic tenor lead singer named Steve Green and an amazing guitar player named Dann Huff, who also had a great, gruff singing voice. Their innovative Christian rock reminded me of the secular group Toto, which was very big at the time. I thought, *How could everyone else have missed this?* But I was glad to have a part in helping them get their music out and succeed. As executive producer on their first album, I helped select and mix their songs. To this day, I consider White Heart the best Christian pop/rock group ever. They had too many hits to list, and remained active for several years, even as many of the original members left the group.

With all their talent, it was no surprise that they all did well. Steve Green has had a long, brilliant solo career and been very active in ministry. Dann Huff went to

Los Angeles with his brother David, who was White Heart's drummer. They formed a new group called *Giant*, which was quite successful on A&M records. And Dann became the number-one session guitarist in L.A. You can hear his work on songs by Michael Jackson, Amy Grant, Roger Hodgson, Steven Curtis Chapman, Juice Newton, Michael W. Smith, George Benson, Whitney Houston, Barbra Streisand and Kenny Rogers. Then Dann moved back to his hometown of Nashville and had phenomenal success as a producer, working with artists such as Faith Hill, Carrie Underwood, Keith Urban, Rascal Flatts and Lonestar.

## The Me Nobody Knows

Another music baby that had a hard time finding its place was a song called *The Me Nobody Knows*, by writer Vincent Grimes. It was among the hundreds of cassettes I was receiving every week. But this song had a unique melody and an especially powerful message—that *God knows me as no one else does*, and that creates a special bond. It hit me immediately as a great song for someone. I called Vincent and said, "Hey, I really love this song. I'd like to publish it." With a publishing arrangement, I knew I'd be able to use my connections to get the song recorded, and then he could start making some money from it. We signed a publishing deal, and then a year went by.

Finally, he called me. "Anything happen with my song?"

"No. I just haven't found the right place yet."

Another year. Still no activity.

Three years. I told him, "No, I'm still looking. But trust me, this is a number-one song!"

Finally, *nine years* went by with nothing to show for this poor writer's efforts. He must have thought he'd been swindled for sure! I know I would have. But then I got a call from a man named Neil Joseph. He had been an executive at Word Music and was now heading up the first Christian label for Warner Brothers, called *Warner Alliance*. Neil said,

"I need a big record to launch this new label. Do you know anybody we could sign?"

I told him, "Well, you know, I did this song, *Safe*, with Steve Archer and Marilyn McCoo. And CCM magazine called it one of the top ten Christian songs of the decade. Let me call Marilyn and see if she'd like to do a solo album."

That led to Marilyn McCoo's first Christian album, on Warner Alliance. And as the producer, I helped her pick the songs. One of the songs I played her was *The Me Nobody Knows*. But as we listened to the demo tape together, she wasn't convinced. "I don't hear it," she said. Marilyn was hearing the rough sound of a piano-voice demo recording. I was hearing the finished record in my head—the record I thought I could produce. Finally, she made me an offer. "If you can guarantee me this will be a number one song," she said, "I'll record it."

That was a tall order. But I said, "Yes, Marilyn, I guarantee you—this will be a number one record!" That's how convinced I was about this song's potential with Marilyn as the vocalist. Marilyn did a remarkable performance on the track but now I had a big burden on my shoulders. If this was to be a number one record, I needed to bring in the best mixing engineer in the business. That meant my old Chilean friend from the Cotton, Lloyd and Christian days—Humberto Gatica. I hadn't talked with Humberto for years, but he agreed to come and mix the record for me. I had to pay him a lot (more, in fact, than it cost to produce the entire Dogwood album), but it was worth it. Humberto gave the recording its special sound. I'm absolutely convinced that without Humberto Gatica engineering the mix, the song would not have done as well as it did.

*The Me Nobody Knows* became the title song of Marilyn's debut Christian album. And yes, it went to number one on the Christian charts and was nominated for a Grammy. Warner Alliance was off to a good start.

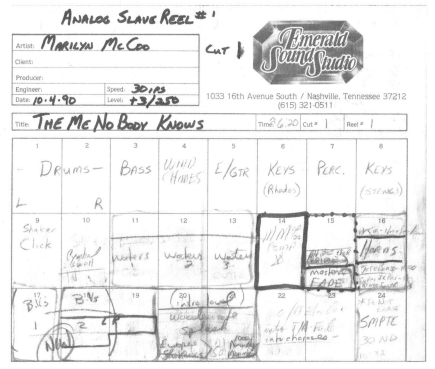

ANALOG SLAVE REEL #1

**Artist:** MARILYN McCOO    CUT 1

**Emerald Sound Studio**

**Client:**

**Producer:**

**Engineer:** | **Speed:** 30 IPS

**Date:** 10·4·90 | **Level:** +3/250

1033 16th Avenue South / Nashville, Tennessee 37212
(615) 321-0511

**Title:** THE ME NO BODY KNOWS    **Time:** 6:20 | **Cut #** 1 | **Reel #** 1

| 1 | 2 | 3 | 4 | 5 | 6 | 7 | 8 |
|---|---|---|---|---|---|---|---|
| — DRUMS — | | BASS | WIND CHIMES | E/GTR | KEYS (Rhodes) | PERC. | KEYS (STRINGS) |
| L | R | | | | | | |
| 9 Shaker Click | 10 Cymbal Swell | 11 waters | 12 waters 2 | 13 waters 3 | 14 | 15 | 16 Horns |
| 17 B'Vs 1 | 18 B'Vs 2 | 19 | 20 | 22 | 23 | 24 SMPTE 30 ND |

# 21

# Things that Shouldn't Have Happened

As I recount all the extraordinary blessings I've received in my life, I feel like a child standing outside a window. The window is cracked open slightly and I'm listening to my own words coming from inside. And as I listen, I'm amazed. *Are you kidding? That happened? And that, too? Are you kidding me?*

Because in my mind, I'm still that little kid from Abilene, the boy in blue jeans, tennis shoes and a T-shirt. That boy dreamed of doing big things—of creating music, making records, and having a song on the radio like Dow Patterson. But the journey God took me on was beyond my imagination.

How likely is it that a regular kid in a medium-sized Texas town would find worldwide success in the music business? Not very. How likely is it that the same kid would write a song in high school—and have it recorded by the biggest star in the world? Or, discover a sixteen-year-old girl who isn't looking for a record deal—and ends up selling 40 million records?

These things *should not have happened*. But they did.

Looking back, I see so many examples like this that it's hard to count them all. I think back to my teen years in Abilene, when I got to shuttle the big music acts around town. What a great opportunity that was! And then, getting a full-ride scholarship at college—for playing music! That was an incredible blessing all by itself. Meeting and working with Archie Campbell, Chet Atkins and Jerry Reed was the kind of break most aspiring musicians in Nashville would give anything for. And those friendships opened so many more doors than I could have opened on my own. How about getting hired to play for the top entertainer in Las Vegas—without ever playing a lick! *These things should not have happened.* But they did.

I've mentioned the three great things that happened to me at a theme park called Opryland—I got to make a living playing music, I got connected with Wayne Newton, and best of all, I met Shanon, the love of my life. That would have been enough to praise God for. But He had a whole lot more in store.

When I heard a group called Dogwood and decided to record them, I couldn't have imagined that it would lead to a lifelong career as a producer. Or that my second project would be with one of the greatest pop singers in the world—BJ Thomas.

To get a call out of the blue to put together the first recording session for Olivia Newton-John in the United States and then write a song for her album, this *should not have happened.* But it did.

Lots of songwriters eventually have their songs recorded. And that first time is always a thrill. But how many have that first song recorded by the king of rock and roll?

And moving to Los Angeles with few contacts—then getting a record deal with a music legend and working with the best producer in the business? Again, these things *shouldn't have happened.* But they did. I've been blessed beyond measure, over and over again.

So, I often ask the question. *Why me, Lord?* It certainly wasn't because I was especially good or virtuous—my wife could tell you that. Some would say I was just lucky. But I don't believe that either. No, I have to go back to Abilene, to the 1950s and my dear godly grandmother, who prayed for me day after day. And it's clear to me that God was answering her prayers.

## Go Global or Go Home!

You see, when Monkey prayed for me to "go into all the world" with the gospel, my child's mind couldn't quite grasp what that meant. But I internalized the part about "all the world." Throughout my life, I've felt that anything I do should be big—on a worldwide scale. And that's how I approached all my endeavors. I never wanted to do anything small. If I couldn't do it in a big way, I didn't want to do it. My wife Shanon reminds me, "You don't have to go global with everything! There are important people to reach right here on our own block." And she's absolutely right. But that drive to go big is just something that's in my DNA. And over the years God allowed me to do some big things.

Through music, I was able to reach people around the world. Sure, He used my own music, but He especially used the music of all the great Christian artists I worked with: Dogwood. Amy Grant. BJ Thomas. White Heart. Steve Archer. Marilyn McCoo. B.W. Stevenson. Dan Peek. The Imperials. Eric Champion. The Boones. Bill Gaither. Pat Boone. Mark Heard. And through their music, the gospel really has gone out into all the world. I couldn't see that while it was happening. It was all going too fast. I was on a train moving 150 miles an hour and I didn't want to think about it because I didn't want it to stop. I was always thinking about the next project or how to meet the next deadline. But now it's clear. God heard the prayers of a godly woman in Abilene, Texas, all those years ago—and answered them abundantly over several decades. Of course, with the Internet, that music is now reaching even more people. It really *is* going into *all* the world. How amazing is that?

## Being the Launch Pad

As a producer, I always saw myself as a launch pad. I could launch artists on their journey; what happened to them after that was in God's hands, and theirs. Amy Grant was a missile destined to reach the stars. I helped launch her amazing career. The launch pad may have said *Home Sweet Home Productions*. But the name on the missile was always *Amy Grant*. That's the way it was with so many artists. I was privileged to serve as their launch pad. And it was gratifying then to see them reach millions with their message and go on to long, effective music careers.

## Just Believe

God doesn't need us to fulfill his plans. But He does tell us to have faith—to believe in Him. The wonderful godly upbringing I received taught me that God is good and powerful, and that He answers prayer. And I believed it. I could only do as much as God would allow me to do; and for all my faults, I have *never* gone to bed without thanking God for everything He has done for me.

The book of James tells us, "The prayer of a righteous person is powerful and effective" (James 5:16 NIV). We're all going to fail sometimes, but if we're thankful and believe in Him, I believe He will bless us and answer our prayers. When we see our own children trying to do the right thing, we're likely to do anything we can to help them. God, our Father, is like that too. Jesus Himself said, "If you, then, though you are evil, know how to give good gifts to your children, how much more will your Father in heaven give good gifts to those who ask him!" (Matthew 7:11 NIV). God wants to do good for us. I always accepted that, and it has proven true in my life.

My message to anyone who will hear it is this: Be encouraged! God really does answer prayer. Keep praying and believe that He will answer you. Pray for your family, your friends, your children, your grandchildren. You might just be amazed.

# 22

# Since You Asked

Occasionally I'm invited to speak at colleges, churches or business seminars. People are interested in my music career, or they've heard about some of my other ventures. It's true, I've invested in several projects and learned a lot about businesses outside of music. Some of them did well, others not so well. But I never felt I was particularly good at those things. I've come to realize that what I really need to do is make music—*because that's what I do*. At those speaking engagements, people usually have specific things they want to know. So rather than talking for fifty minutes and answering questions for ten, I've found it more effective to simply invite their questions and answer them.

One of the most common questions I hear is *How do you handle rejection?* It seems that's a big issue for a lot of folks, especially young musicians and songwriters. When I first heard it, I wasn't sure how to answer. "I've never been rejected," I said. That drew a laugh; they thought I was joking. But I wasn't trying to be flippant. I really couldn't recall ever experiencing rejection. As I thought about it later, I realized I *had* been rejected. I just didn't interpret it that way. After all, on that first trip to Nashville I was walking up and down Music Row, hearing *no* over and over again. But somehow it didn't register as rejection. I just figured they weren't all that smart or didn't have good ears. So I kept going. To a large degree, that attitude came from my upbringing. I've mentioned how my grandmother's prayers shaped my life and how my dad's encouragement sent me on my way to Nashville. But the others in my family were also wonderfully supportive. My mother thought

I could do no wrong. To her, everything I did was phenomenal. If I wrote a song, it was the greatest song she'd ever heard. She'd have the ladies over to play cards and say, "Oh, Chris, come out and play that beautiful song you wrote." When I set up my Ludwig drum set in the house and began making a horrible racket that sounded like World War III, she'd come in and say, "Oh, that was wonderful! I loved it." So I developed a confidence that whatever I was doing was phenomenal. And I think that shielded me from the pain of rejection that so many people experience.

That's a good lesson for us parents and grandparents. Encouragement can do wonders for our children. We have the power to put a lid on their dreams—or open the sky up to them. What we instill in them, good or bad, will last a lifetime. And they'll likely pass on those same lessons on to their kids.

I'm not writing this as someone who has done everything right. As the years have passed, I've realized some of the many areas where I fell short. When I was raising my kids, I followed my dad's example and tried to show love through my actions. I don't remember my dad ever saying, *I love you*, until his later years. But I never doubted his love for a second. He showed it every day by being there to support me, coming to every game and every recital. And that was how I related to my kids. But later I realized it wasn't enough. My daughter once told me, "Dad, you never asked me how I *felt*." That hit me hard. I had raised her like a guy—the way I was raised. But she needed more from me, and I hadn't given it to her. Likewise, when I was starting in the music business, I was consumed with my work. And I wasn't always aware of how it was affecting my wife. She needed me to be there for her, and often I was too busy to see her pain. I felt I needed to keep working hard, because I knew some new producer could show up in Nashville at any moment and my good fortune could end. I didn't want to squander the great opportunities I'd been given. But I lost precious moments with the one I loved most. So, my message to husbands and parents is—don't blow it like I did! Take time to cherish your loved ones. Don't let the *urgent* smother the *important*. And if you have daughters, ask them how they're feeling every now and then.

## How to Get Ahead

It's amazing to me to think of all the great people I've met simply by walking up and talking with them—from entertainers to politicians. For some reason, important people never intimidated me. And somehow, I understood that the way to get anywhere was to meet folks who were already there. It sounds simple, but I see a lot of young people who don't think that way. And I wonder if they'll ever achieve all they could have. If you want to be CEO of Exxon, Amazon or Google, try to meet somebody who works there. If you can, meet the CEO! But get to know somebody. You might meet the vice president—who can then one day introduce you to the CEO.

And then—be nice! Do everything you can for that person, expect nothing in return, and you might just be on your way to doing what YOU want to do.

## Family Legacy

It seems like yesterday that I was standing at the bottom of a billboard on Sunset Boulevard, looking up at a huge image of Cotton, Lloyd and Christian. Today I'm standing in the yard playing catch with my grandsons.

One day I said to my dad, "You've been such an encouragement and support for me growing up. How can I ever pay you back?"

He said something I'll never forget: "Just do the same thing for your children."

I followed my dad's example as well as I could. And now that I'm a grandfather, I'm hoping to repay my grandmother for all she did for me—by doing the same for my grandchildren. Grandparents do things for their grandchildren mostly out of unconditional love, not obligation. And I hope I can give the love, support, and encouragement to my grandchildren that my grandmother gave to me.

## Keys to Success

Once I was at a seminar at a university and heard the speaker before me encourage the young students to *follow their opportunities*. That seemed to make sense and a lot of people nodded. But when my turn came to speak, I respectfully disagreed. "If I had followed my opportunities, I'd be working at the bank today," I told them. "Instead, I followed my passion—to make music." That choice made all the difference. When I took off for Nashville that first time, I had no existing opportunities. I didn't know how the music business worked. I didn't know any songwriters. I didn't know how to make records. I just knew that music was my passion. I'd been writing songs since the fourth grade—not as a path to success, but because it was something I had to do. And by following my passion, I was able to create music that reached the world. I was an ordinary guy who had extraordinary things happen to him. And even when things didn't work out, I still enjoyed the ride.

Listen to those with more experience than you. Sometimes, a simple word or sentence they say can change your life. Once I was in small Bible study in our home with two of my great friends, Steve Reinemund and Jim Beckett. As the guy in charge of the topic that evening, I said I wanted to talk about how important it is to live a balanced life. Steve, whom I respect as much as anyone I've ever known said, "Excuse me, but I think that's nonsense." I asked him to explain. "A balanced life is a life of mediocrity," he continued. "You do everything average if you try to do everything".

So, I said, "Then what is it"?

He said, *"I think it is a life of priorities."*

He was right. Up until that moment, I had been aiming at the wrong target my whole life. What is a life of priorities? It's simple: *One, two, three.* Identify your top priority and pursue that relentlessly. Then, your next priority, and then the third. That's a key to success.

Failure? You haven't failed until you quit. Until then, you're not failing—you're just changing.

These are some things I've learned over forty years in the rough and tumble world of music and business. I hope they'll help and encourage you.

And I hope you'll never quit praying.

Please visit www.grandmothersprayer.com for additional resources, more images, the backstory behind the color images in this book, and to share your "Grandmother's Prayer" story.

# Lessons Learned

I'm not sure these thoughts are any better than anyone else's. But for what it's worth, here's a summary of the lessons I've learned:

1. Pray. God answers the prayers of anyone who wants to follow His will.

2. Go where people are doing what you want to do. Find someone who's doing it. Then, do everything you can for that person—expecting nothing in return.

3. Listen twice as much as you talk. Remember, you have only one mouth, but two ears.

4. The goal is not a balanced life; that's the path to mediocrity. The goal is a life of priorities.

5. Follow your passion, not your opportunities.

6. Identify your target as specifically as possible. Remember, if you aim for nothing you'll hit it every time!

7. Make sure all your daily choices are getting you closer to what you want to do and who you want to be.

8. At the end of the day, the only important things are family and friends. Learn this early.

9. Despite what people say, it's not *who you know* that leads to success. It's *who likes you.*

10. Try to understand each person's love language. It may not be the same as yours.

11. Keep the main thing the main thing.

12. Cherish moments of time, not just accomplishments.

13. Ask questions of those older than you. And then, listen.

14. Nothing good lasts. And nothing bad lasts.

15. Big men have the time. Little men are too busy.

16. Life is short, art is long.

17. The road to success is not a ladder, it's a jungle gym.

18. If it isn't on video, it did not happen. © CCEntertainment LLC.

If nothing else, this book represents a few examples of how God has answered prayers in my life—from a loving grandmother, and a young boy that continued his grandmother's prayers. I've walked through my life under the umbrella of her prayers. The things that happened for me and to me should not have happened. I did try to work harder than most. I tried to give everything I could in everything I did. And I tried to keep the *important* in front of the *urgent*. I didn't always succeed, but I always tried, at least after I was thirty years old. I think before then I had tunnel vision.

If you are a grandparent, the other thing I hope you take away from this book is to pray for your grandchildren daily. You will change your grandchildren's lives, and who knows, because of that, you might also change the WORLD.

To all: There is a God, there is a plan for your life, and there is a purpose for which you were born. Find it!

**My life would have turned out so differently
if not for the answers to *my grandmother's prayers*.**

# Appendix

**THE INTERNATIONAL NEWSWEEKLY OF MUSIC AND HOME ENTERTAINMENT**

OCTOBER 5, 1985/$3.50 (U.S.)

## GOSPEL LECTERN
*by Bob Darden*

**M**UCH HAS BEEN WRITTEN and said about **Amy Grant's** incredible success in both Christian and mainstream markets—and rightly so. But **Chris Christian** got there first.

Christian was the first artist to come out of contemporary Christian music to both write and perform mainstream top 40 hits. Today he is the focal point of the second largest music-making machine in contemporary Christian music—behind only the legendary **Bill Gaither.** And he's back in the news once again after signing an incredible production deal with **Word Records** for 40 albums over the next four years.

## Christian is comfortable in two different musical worlds

Oh, and one other thing, just to complete the circle: It was Christian and producer **Brown Bannister** who first heard and signed Amy Grant to a Word deal nearly a decade ago.

Fifteen years ago, Christian, **Mike Blanton** (of **Blanton/Harrell Productions**) and Bannister were roommates at Abilene Christian College in Texas, dreaming about the music business. After a stint at Opryland and as a session musician, Christian began to catch the ear of some well-known entertainers.

Soon he was writing for and performing with the likes of Elvis Presley, Olivia Newton-John, Dionne Warwick, Sheena Easton, B.J Thomas and the Carpenters (his "Back In My Life Again" was Karen Carpenter's last single). A trio called **Cotton, Lloyd & Christian** spawned the top 40 single "I Go To Pieces."

About that time, Christian produced **B.J Thomas'** first contemporary Christian album, ("Home Where I Belong," which would go gold and win a Grammy in 1977. In short order, his religious career all but eclipsed his secular career. Other Grammy- and Dove Award-winning albums followed, including **the Imperials'** "Sail On" and **the Boone Sisters'** "First Class."

As a songwriter, Christian penned "Sail On," "All Things Are Possible," "Satisfaction Guaranteed," "Too Late," "Love Them While We Can," "Heed The Call," "Why Does The Devil Have All The Good Music?" and many more.

Since that time, Christian has crossed between both musical genres. On his own, he's recorded two top 20 hits, "I Want You, I Need You" and "Ain't Nothing Like The Real Thing" (as the first artist signed to Neil Bogart's Boardwalk label), and written the hit "All Things Are Possible" for **Dan Peek.**

Today, Christian's business offices are located in Dallas, his creative offices are in Los Angeles, and he has a studio (Gold Mine) and another office in Nashville. In addition to his 15 employees, he has another 11 writers. But rather than tie him down, he says his various operations have freed him up to do what he likes most: finding and producing new talent in both mainstream and Christian music venues.

("God blessed me with the ability to find new artists of merit and give them a platform," he says quietly from his Los Angeles office. "That's always been my history, and I find tremendous enjoyment in that. So after cutting back my work in contemporary Christian music a couple of years ago, I just felt the time was right to return. There was no one thing, but projects by people like **Steve Archer, White Heart, Rick Riso** and **Glen Allen Green** just happened to come along—projects I believed in."

As of December 31, 1980

Kristal Entertainment
1930 Century Park East
5th Floor
Los Angeles, California 90067

Re: <u>Personal Management Agreement</u>

Gentlemen:

I desire to obtain your advice, counsel and direction
in the development and enhancement of all aspects of my
career in the entertainment industry and related fields, without
exception or limitation except as expressly set forth herein.
The nature and extent of the success or failure of my career
cannot be predetermined and it is therefore my desire that
your compensation be determined in such manner as will permit
you to benefit to the extent of my success, but also accept
the risk of failure.

In view of the foregoing, we have agreed as follows:

1. I do hereby engage you as my personal manager.
The term of this Agreement shall commence as of the date set
forth hereinabove and continue for a period of one (1) year.
I grant you four (4) separate consecutive options to extend
this agreement for periods of one (1) year each, said option
periods to run consecutively beginning at the expiration of
the original term or any renewal term upon all of the same
terms and conditions as are applicable to the original term.
Each option shall be deemed to be automatically exercised by
you unless you shall give me written notice at least sixty
(60) days prior to the expiration of the original term or
any renewal period hereunder that you do not desire to exercise
any such option. The original term and option years are
hereinafter referred to as the contract year(s). As and
when requested by me during and throughout the term hereof,
you agree to perform services customarily performed by personal
managers with regard to my activities which are commissionable
by you hereunder in the entertainment industry and related
fields including without limitation as follows: advise and
counsel in the selection of material; advise and counsel in
any and all matters pertaining to publicity, public relations
and advertising; advise and counsel with relation to the
adoption of proper format for presentation of my artistic
talents and in the determination of proper style, mood,
setting, business and characterization in keeping with my

If the foregoing meets with your approval, please indicate
the acceptance of the Agreement by signing in the space
provided below.

Very truly yours,

CHRIS CHRISTIAN

9321 Cherokee Lane,
Los Angeles, California

AGREED TO:

KRISTAL ENTERTAINMENT

By
ROBERT KARDASHIAN d/b/a
KRISTAL ENTERTAINMENT

# TOP 50 Adult Contemporary ™

These are best selling middle-of-the-road singles compiled from radio station air play listed in rank order.

| This Week | Last Week | Weeks on Chart | TITLE, Artist, Label & Number (Dist. Label) (Publisher, Licensee) |
|---|---|---|---|
| ☆ | 3 | 8 | THE OLD SONGS <br> Barry Manilow, Arista 0633 (WB/Upward Spiral, ASCAP) |
| 2 | 1 | 11 | HERE I AM <br> Air Supply, Arista 0626 (Al Gallico/Turtle, BMI) |
| ☆ | 6 | 6 | WHY DO FOOLS FALL IN LOVE <br> Diana Ross, RCA 12349 (Patricia, BMI) |
| 4 | 4 | 11 | THE THEME FROM HILL STREET BLUES <br> Mike Post, Elektra 47186 (MGM, ASCAP) |
| 5 | 5 | 9 | OH NO <br> Commodores, Motown 1527 (Jobete/Commodores Entertainment, ASCAP) |
| ☆ | 9 | 4 | YESTERDAYS SONGS <br> Neil Diamond, Columbia 18-02604 (Stonebridge, ASCAP) |
| ★ | 8 | 7 | WAITING FOR A GIRL LIKE YOU <br> Foreigner, Atlantic 3858 (Somerset/Evensongs, ASCAP) |
| 8 | 2 | 14 | HARD TO SAY <br> Dan Fogelberg, Epic 14-02488 (Hickory Grove/April/Blackwood, ASCAP) |
| ★ | 10 | 8 | I WANT YOU I NEED YOU <br> Chris Christian, Boardwalk 7-11-126 (Marvin Gardens/Home Sweet Home/Bug And Bear, ASCAP/John Charles Crowley, BMI) |
| ☆ | 13 | 6 | CASTLES IN THE AIR <br> Don McLean, Millennium 11819 (RCA) (Mayday/Benny Bird, BMI) |
| ☆ | 14 | 5 | TURN YOUR LOVE AROUND <br> George Benson, Warner Bros. 49846 (Garden Rake/Rehtakul/JSH, ASCAP) |
| ☆ | 16 | 6 | THE SWEETEST THING <br> Juice Newton, Capitol 5046 (Sterling/Addison Street, ASCAP) |
| ☆ | 21 | 3 | COMIN' IN AND OUT OF YOUR LIFE <br> Barbra Streisand, Columbia 18-02621 (Songs Of Bandier-Koppelman/Landers-Whiteside/Emanuel, ASCAP) |
| 14 | 15 | 10 | STEAL THE NIGHT <br> Stevie Woods, Cotillion 46018 (Atlantic) (Sunrise, BMI) |
| ☆ | 19 | 4 | I WOULDN'T HAVE MISSED IT FOR THE WORLD <br> Ronnie Milsap, RCA 12342 (Pi-Gem/Chess, BMI/ASCAP) |
| ☆ | 20 | 6 | HOOKED ON CLASSICS <br> Royal Philharmonic Orchestra, RCA 12304 (Chappell, ASCAP) |
| 17 | 18 | 8 | THE WOMAN IN ME <br> Crystal Gayle, Columbia 02523 (OAS, ASCAP) |
| ☆ | 25 | 4 | LEATHER AND LACE <br> Stevie Nicks With Don Henley, Modern 7341 (Atlantic) (Welsh Witch, BMI) |
| 19 | 7 | 11 | JUST ONCE <br> Quincy Jones Featuring James Ingram, A&M 2357 (ATV/Mann & Weil, BMI) |
| 20 | 12 | 13 | SHARE YOUR LOVE WITH ME <br> Kenny Rogers, Liberty 1430 (Duchess, BMI) |
| 21 | 11 | 12 | WHEN SHE WAS MY GIRL <br> The Four Tops, Casablanca 2338 (MCA, ASCAP) |
| ☆ | 30 | 2 | COOL NIGHT <br> Paul Davis, Arista 9645 (Web IV, BMI) |
| 23 | 17 | 11 | FANCY FREE <br> Oak Ridge Boys, MCA 51169 (Goldline/Silverline, ASCAP/BMI) |
| 24 | 23 | 16 | WE'RE IN THIS LOVE TOGETHER <br> Al Jarreau, Warner Bros. 49746 (Blackwood/Magic Castle, BMI) |
| ☆ | 31 | 4 | TROUBLE <br> Lindsey Buckingham, Asylum 77223 (Elektra) (Now Sounds, BMI) |
| 26 | 24 | 15 | ARTHUR'S THEME <br> Christopher Cross, Warner Bros. 49787 (Irving/Woolnough/Unichappell/Begonia, BMI/Hidden Valley, ASCAP) |
| 27 | 22 | 12 | IT'S ALL I CAN DO <br> Anne Murray, Capitol 5023 (Chess, ASCAP) |
| 28 | 26 | 10 | ATLANTA LADY <br> Marty Balin, EMI-America 8093 (Mercury Shoes/Great Pyramid, BMI) |
| 29 | 27 | 9 | YOU SAVED MY SOUL <br> Burton Cummings, Alfa 7008 (Shillelagh, BMI) |
| ☆ | NEW ENTRY | | SOMEONE COULD LOSE A HEART TONIGHT <br> Eddie Rabbitt, Elektra 47239 (Briarpatch/Debdave, BMI) |
| ★ | 35 | 3 | IF I WERE YOU <br> Lulu, Alfa 7011 (Blackwood/Fullness, BMI) |
| ★ | 37 | 2 | MORE THAN JUST THE TWO OF US <br> Sneaker, Handshake 9-02557 (Shellsongs/Sneaker/Home Grown, BMI) |
| 33 | 33 | 3 | PRIVATE EYES <br> Daryl Hall & John Oates, RCA 12290 (Fust Buzza/Hot-Cha/Six Continents, BMI) |
| ☆ | NEW ENTRY | | COME GO WITH ME <br> The Beach Boys, Caribou 5-02633 (Epic) (Gil/See Bee, BMI) |
| 35 | 29 | 5 | PHYSICAL <br> Olivia Newton-John, MCA 51182 (Stephen A. Kippner/April/Terry Shaddick, ASCAP/BMI) |
| ★ | NEW ENTRY | | I CAN'T GO FOR THAT <br> Daryl Hall & John Oates, RCA 12361 (Fust Buzza/Hot-Cha/Six Continents, BMI) |
| ★ | NEW ENTRY | | SHE'S GOT A WAY <br> Billy Joel, Columbia 18-02628 (April/Impulsive, ASCAP) |
| 38 | 36 | 8 | I SURRENDER <br> Arlan Day, Pasha 5-02480 (CBS) (WB/Pasha/Hovona, ASCAP) |
| 39 | 32 | 18 | STEP BY STEP <br> Eddie Rabbitt, Elektra 47174 (Briarpatch/DebDave, BMI) |
| ★ | NEW ENTRY | | LOVED BY THE ONE YOU LOVE <br> Rupert Holmes, Elektra 47225 (WB/The Holmes Line, ASCAP) |
| 41 | 42 | 4 | NOBODY KNOWS ME LIKE YOU |

# CHRIS CHRISTIAN'S SONGWRITING AND PRODUCING CREDITS

### The Carpenters
From the " Made In America" album
"Back In My Life Again" (Chris Christian, Kerry Chater)

### Olivia Newton John
From the "Don't Stop Believing" album
"Compassionate Man" (Chris Christian, John Farrar)

### Elvis Presley
From the " Promised Land" album"
"Love Song of the Year" (Chris Christian)

### Dionne Warwick
From the " No Night So Long" album
"When the World Runs Out of Love" (Chris Christian, Robbie Patton)

### Sheena Easton
From the "You Could of Been With Me" Album
"Telephone Lines" (Chris Christian, Steve Kipner)

### B.J. Thomas
From the "Home Where I Belong" Album
"Without a Doubt" (Chris Christian, BJ Thomas)
"You Were There To Catch Me" (Chris Christian, Archie Jordan)
"Down Isn't So Bad" (Chris Christian)
"Starving Sinner, Sleeping Saint" (Chris Christian)
"Common Ground" (Chris Christian, Archie Jordon)

From the MCA Records Pop album
"Still The Lovin Is Fun" (Chris Christian)
"My Love" (Chris Christian)
"Plastic Words" (Chris Christian, Archie Jordan)

From the "For The Best" album
"Everything Always Works Out For The Best" (Chris Christian, Lewis Anderson)
"Walking On A Cloud" (Chris Christian)
"The Faith That Only Comes From You" (Chris Christian)

From the " BJ Thomas in Concert" Album
"Walking On A Cloud" (Chris Christian)
"The Faith That Comes From You" (Chris Christian)
"Everything Always Works Out For The Best" (Chris Christian, Lewis Anderson)

From the "On This Christmas Night' Album
"God Bless the Children" (Chris Christian)
"On This Christmas Night" (Chris Christian)

From the "Best of BJ Thomas" Album
"Without A Doubt" (Chris Christian)

From the "BJ Thomas Best of 2" Album
"Odessa Beggarman" (Chris Christian)

**Dan Peek**
From the "All Things Are Possible" album
"All Things Are Possible" (Chris Christian, Dan Peek)
"Ready For Love" (Chris Christian, Dan Peek)
"Love Was Just Another Word" (Chris Christian, Steve Kipner)
"One Way" (Chris Christian)

From the "Doer of the World" Album
"Everything" (Chris Christian, Phil Naish, Dan Peek)
"Brotherly Love" (Chris Christian, Dan Peek)
"Your Father Love You" (Chris Christian)

**Marilyn McCoo**
From the "The Me Nobody Knows" Album
"The Me Nobody Knows" (Vincent Grimes, Chris Christian)
"Just Before You Go" (Chris Christian)
"Against The Wall" (Chris Christian)
"One Way Conversation" (Chris Christian)

"White Christmas" Album

**B.W. Stevenson**
From the "Lifeline" Album
"Holding A Special Place for You" (Chris Christian, B.W. Stevenson)
"Lifeline" (Chris Christian, B.W. Stevenson)
"Show Me The Way to the City" (Chris Christian, B.W. Stevenson)
"You Were There" (Chris Christian, B.W. Stevenson)
"Paradise" (Chris Christian, B.W. Stevenson)
"There is Someone Who Loves You" (Chris Christian)
"One True Way" (Chris Christian, B.W. Stevenson)
"Headed Home" (Chris Christian)

**Amy Grant**
From the "Never Alone" Album
"So Glad" (Brown Bannister, Amy Grant, Chris Christian)
"Walking Away With You" (Chris Christian, Gary Chapman, Amy Grant)
"It's a Miracle" (Chris Christian, Gary Chapman)
"Too Late" (Chris Christian, Brown Bannister, Amy Grant)
Others:
Santa's Reindeer Ride (Reba Rambo, Chris Christian)

**Donnie Osmond**
From the "Disco Train" album
"Reaching for the Feeling" (Chris Christian)

**Donnie and Marie Osmond**

From the "Songs from their Television Show" album
"Sunshine Lady" (Chris Christian)

**Jerry Reed**

From the "Uptown Poker Club" Album
"Lay it on My Lady" (Chris Christian)

From the "A Good Woman's Love" Album
"Hurry Home" (Chris Christian)

**Little Anthony**
From the "Daylight" Album
"Love's The Only Way To Survive" (Chris Christian, Brown Bannister)
"My Best Friend" (Chris Christian, Michael Hanna, Milton Blackford)

**Cheryl Ladd**
From the" Fascinated" album
"Lesson From The Leavin" (Brian Russell, Chris Christian)

### Jane Olivor
From the "Stay the Night" album
"Can't Leave You, Cause I Love You" (Chris Christian)

### Ali Lohan
From the "Lohan Holiday" album
"Christmas Day" (Chris Christian)
"I Like Christmas" (Chris Christian, Nigel George)
"Lohan Holiday" (Chris Christian, Nigel George, Keith Nelson)
"Santa's Reindeer Ride" (Reba Rambo, Chris Christian)

### Imperials
From the "Sail On" album
"Sail On" (Chris Christian)
"Satisfaction Guaranteed" (Chris Christian)

From the "Heed The Call" album
"Heed The Call" (Chris Christian)
"First Morning In Heaven" (Chris Christian)

### The Boone Girls
From the" First Class" album
"I'm a Believer" (Chris Christian)
"My Love Will Never Change" (Chris Christian)
"Caught In This World" (Chris Christian)
"Let Me Be Lonely" (Chris Christian)
"Perfect Love" (Chris Christian)

From the" Heavenly Love" album
"Heavenly Love" (Chris Christian)
"No I've Never" (Chris Christian, Lanier Ferguson)
"You Came Softly" (Chris Christian)
"No I Can't Stop" (Chris Christian)

From the" Highlights" album

"No, I've Never" (Chris Christian, Lanier Ferguson)
"I'm a Believer" (Chris Christian)
"Heavenly Love" (Chris Christian)
"My Love Will Never Change" (Chris Christian)
"You Came Softly" (Chris Christian)
"Please Be Patient With Me" (Chris Christian)
"No, I Can't Stop" (Chris Christian)

Christmas

"Gift of Love" (Chris Christian, Shanon Smith)

### Cotton, Lloyd &Christian
From the "The "Cotton, Lloyd & Christian" album
"I Don't Know Why You Love Me" (Chris Christian)
"Robot Man" (Chris Christian)
"Love Me Away" (Chris Christian)

From the "Cotton, Lloyd & Christian II" album
"Childhood Dreams" (Chris Christian)
"Buffalo" (Chris Christian)

From the Soundtrack to the movie "The Pom Pom Girls"
"Robot Man" (Chris Christian)
"Love Me Away" (Chris Christian)

### Darryl Cotton
From the "Best Seat In The House" album
"Darlin" (Chris Christian, Robbie Patton)
"Same Old Girl" (Chris Christian, Darryl Cotton) #1 Austrailia
"Here Comes Another Heartache" (Chris Christian, Darryl Cotton)
"Hollywood" (Chris Christian, Darryl Cotton)

## Chris Christian

From the "Chris Christian" album
"Why Does The Devil Have All The Good Music" (Chris Christian)
"Mountain Top" (Chris Christian)
"Starving Sinner, Sleeping Saint" (Chris Christian)
"Odessa Beggarman" (Chris Christian)
"Hallelujah" (Shanon Smith, Chris Christian)
"Get Back To The Bible" (Chris Christian)
"Great, Great, Joy" (Chris Christian)
"Grave Cave" (Chris Christian)
"You Are Love" (Chris Christian)
"I Don't Deserve" (Chris Christian)

From the "Chance" album

"Now I See The Man" (Chris Christian)
"Satisfaction Guaranteed" (Chris Christian)
"Passing Through" (Chris Christian)
"Please, Please" (Chris Christian)
"From The Start" (Chris Christian)

From the "With Your Love" album

"With Your Love" (Chris Christian)
"Already Livin' In Heaven" (Chris Christian, Shanon Smith)
"You Are The One Love I Need" (Chris Christian)
"Sunday Words" (Chris Christian)
"Fine Love" (Chris Christian)
"Love's The Only Way To Survive" (Chris Christian Brown Bannister)
"Heed The Call" (Chris Christian, Shanon Smith)
"Pray Away" (Chris Christian, Shanon Smith)

From the "Love Them While We Can" album

"Put Your Trust" (Chris Christian)
"We're Our Only Captain" (Chris Christian)
"Too Heavenly Minded" (Chris Christian)
"One Man's Toy" (Chris Christian)
"Why Are We First" (Chris Christian)
"Pray For Me Always" (Chris Christian)

From the "Let The Music Start" album

"Blessed Be The Lord" (Chris Christian)
"Selah" (Chris Christian)

From the "Higher Ways" album

"Love Did It" (Chris Christian)
"Day Like Today" (Chris Christian)
"Still In Love" (Chris Christian)
"Please, Please" (Chris Christian)
"He Won't Unlove You" (Chris Christian, Steve Kipner)

From the "Mirror Of Your Heart" album

"Mirror of Your Heart" (Chris Christian)
"From The Start" (Chris Christian)
"Look How Far You've Come" (Chris Christian, Jamie Owens Collins)
"Pray Away" (Chris Christian)

From the "No Lyrics" album

"Genesis" (Chris Christian)
"February 7$^{th}$" (Chris Christian)
"Dakota's Theme" (Chris Christian)
"Nighttime Skyline" (Chris Christian)
"Shanon's Song" (Chris Christian)
"Max" (Chris Christian)
"Father And Son" (Chris Christian)
"Trinity Road" (Chris Christian)
"The Chase" (Chris Christian)
"Soda Shop" (Chris Christian)
"Revelation" (Chris Christian)

A Grandmother's Prayer

From the "Sketches" album

"Santa Barbara" (Chris Christian)
"Superbowl Highlights" (Chris Christian)
"Malibu Rain" (Chris Christian)
"Nashville" (Chris Christian)
"Windmills In The Desert" (Chris Christian)
"Sketches In The Sand" (Chris Christian)
"Casey Noel" (Chris Christian)
"Nobody Knows" (Chris Christian)
"Preston Road" (Chris Christian)
"Leaves On The Green" (Chris Christian)
"Court Wants a Pup" (Chris Christian)
"Playin' Catch" (Chris Christian)

From the "Chris Christian (POP)" album

"Don't Give Up On Us" (Chris Christian, JC Crowley)
"I Want You, I Need You" (Chris Christian, JC Crowley)
"Love's Not One To Forget" (Chris Christian, Kerry Chater. Shanon Smith, Brad Smith)
"The Last Goodbye" (Chris Christian, JC Crowley)
"Make It Last" (Chris Christian, JC Crowley)
"Houston" (Chris Christian, J C Crowley)
"I Don't Believe You" (Chris Christian, JC Crowley)
"What Can There Be" (Chris Christian)
"Whatever It Is" (Chris Christian, JC Crowley)
"Deja Vous" (Chris Christian, David Martin)
"Walnut Hill" (Chris Christian)
"Only Wanna Be With You" (Chris Christian, David Martin)
"Day Like Today" (Chris Christian, Jeremy Dalton)
"Santa Barbara" (Chris Christian)

From the "Harbour" album
"Don't Tell Me You Love Me" (David Martin, Chris Christian)
"Unlove Me' (Steve Kipner, Chris Christian)
"Back In My Life Again" (Chris Christian, Kerry Chater)
"Harbour" (Chris Christian, Kenny Passarelli)
"Radio" (Chris Christian)
"I Can't Leave You Cause I Love You" (Chris Christian)
"Lover's Lullabye" (Chris Christian)
"Truly Yours" (Chris Christian)

" The Collection, Vol. 1 1976-1981" album
" The Collection, Vol. 2 1983-1991" album

**Robbie Patton-Chris Christian**
From the "Back In The Day" album
"Darlin (this time girl) (Chris Christian, Robbie Patton)
"Back In The Day" (Chris Christian, Robbie Patton)
"Walking On Air" (Chris Christian, Robbie Patton)
"More" (Chris Christian, Robbie Patton)
"What Can There Be" (Chris Christian)
"Only Wanna Be With You" (Chris Christian, David Martin)
"Do You Wanna Tonight" (Chris Christian, Robbie Patton)
"Last Goodbye" (Chris Christian, JC Crowley)
"Never Coming Down" (Chris Christian, Robbie Patton)
"Make It Last" (Chris Christian, JC Crowley)
"Cheap Wine and Dancing" (Chris Christian, Robbie Patton)
"No Time, This Time" (Chris Christian, Robbie Patton)
"Shouldn't Do It" (Chris Christian, Robbie Patton)
"Cheap Wine and Dancing" (Chris Christian, Robbie Patton)
"I Don't Want To Know It" (Chris Christian, Robbie Patton)
"If This Is It" (Chris Christian, Robbie Patton)
"No Time Next Time" (Chris Christian, Robbie Patton)
"When The World Runs Out Of Love" (Chris Christian, Robbie Patton)
"Why Don't You Answer" (Chris Christian, Robbie Patton)
"You Shouldn't Do It" (Chris Christian, Robbie Patton)

**Robbie Patton**
From the "Do You Wanna Tonight" album
Darlin' *this time girl* (Chris Christian, Robbie Patton)
No Time – This Time (Chris Christian, Robbie Patton)
Do you Wanna Tonight (Chris Christian, Robbie Patton)
No Cheap Wine and Dancing (Chris Christian, Robbie Patton)
Never Comin' Down (Chris Christian, Robbie Patton)

**Steve Archer**
From the "Solo" album
"Living In This Hands" (Steve Bower/Chris Christian)
"He's Coming Back For Me" (Chris Christian)
"But You Didn't" (Chris Christian, Gary McSpadden)
"Unto Me" (Chris Christian, Billy Masters)

From the "Through His Eyes" album
"Blood of Jesus" (Chris Christian, Shanon Smith, Mike Barnes)

From the "Off The Page" album
"Off The Page" (Chris Christian, Gary Floyd)

"Action" album

**Luke Garrett**
From the "Luke Garrett" album
"Judgement In The Gate" (Chris Christian)
"Then Came The Morning" (Chris Christian, Bill Gaither)

From the "Every Constant Ever Sure" album
"My God" (Chris Christian)
"The Love That Once Was There" (Chris Christian, Luke Garrett)
"I Love You Still" (Chris Christian, Tony Sutherland)

From the "Fine Joy" album
"I Remember The Time" (Chris Christian)

**Rick Riso**
"Gotta Have The Real Thing" album

"Shouting At The Walls" album

**Austin Roberts**
From the "Paint My Life" album
" I Have Never Sung With Angels" (Chris Christian, Austin Roberts)
"The Perfect Stranger" (Chris Christian, Austin Roberts)

**David Meece**
From the "I Just Call On You" album
"It's Gonna Be So Lovely" (Chris Christian, David Meece)

**David Martin**
"Stronger Than The Weight" album

**Gaither Vocal Band and Bill Gaither Trio**
"Where Would I Turn" (Chris Christian)
"He Came Down to My Level" - (Chris Christian, Dwight Liles)
"Not by Might, Not by Power" (Chris Christian, Bill Gaither)
"Abide In Me" (Chris Christian, Bill Gaither)
"Living Sacrifice" (Chris Christian, Dwight Liles)
"Then Came The Morning"- (Chris Christian, Bill & Gloria Gaither)
"I'm Somebody" (Chris Christian, Bill Gaither)

**Jamie Owens-Collins**
From the "Straight Ahead" album
"Look How Far You've Come" (Chris Christian, Jamie Owens-Collins)

A Grandmother's Prayer

**Sandi Patti**
From the "Make His Praise Glorious" album
"No Other Name" (Chris Christian, Gary McSpadden, Billy Smiley)

**Steve Flanigan**
From the "Lead the Way" album
"The Blood of Jesus" (Chris Christian, Michael Barnes)
"He Came Down to My Level" - (Chris Christian, Dwight Liles)

**Lynn Sutter**
From the "Everlasting Love" album

"Everlasting Kind of Love" (Chris Christian)
"More of You" (Chris Christian, Shanon Smith)
"Make Me Smile" (Chris Christian, Brown Bannister)
"Heed the Call" (Chris, Shanon Smith)
"No Greater Love" (Chris Christian)
"Satisfaction Guaranteed" (Chris Christian)
"I Love You" (Chris Christian)
"Break Out" (Chris, Shanon Smith)

**Glen Allen Green**
"A Living Fire" album
"Down This Avenue" album

**Lanier Fergusion**
From the "Nothing Could Be Better" album
"No, I've Never" (Chris Christian, Lanier Ferguson)

**Tami Gunden**
"Written On My Heart" album

**Michael James Murphy**
"No Kidnap Today" album

**Honeytree in Concert**
"Me and My Guitar" album

**Three in One**
"Built To Last" album

**Worship**
"We Have Gaithered At This Place" (Chris Christian)
"Search Me" (Chris Christian)

**Star Shower**
Chris Christian, Jack Puig (CCM medleys)

**On This Christmas Night**

"On This Christmas Night" (Chris Christian)
"God Bless The Children" (Chris Christian)
"Gift of Love" (Chris Christian, Shanon Smith)
"Santa's Reindeer Ride" (Chris Christian, Reba Rambo)

**Dallas Cowboys Christmas 85**

"I Don't Want To Be Home Christmas" (Chris Christian)
"God Bless The Children" (Chris Christian)
"It's Christmas Time" (Chris Christian)
"Christmas All Year Round" (Chris Christian)
"On This Christmas Night" (Chris Christian)

**Dallas Cowboys Christmas 86**

"Living The American Dream" (Chris Christian, Bob Bruenig)
"Good Ole Days" (Chris Christian, Bob Bruenig)
"Thinking Of You This Christmas" (Chris Christian)
"Christmas in Dallas" (Chris Christian)
"Gift of Love" (Chris Christian, Shanon Smith)

**Home Sweet Home Christmas**

**We Are His Hands**

**Contemporary Christmas Classics**


**Alvin Stardust**
From the "A Picture Of You" album
" (Want You) Back In My Life Again" (Chris Christian, Kerry Chater)

**The Wynners**
From the "Project 88" album
"I Don't Know Why You Love Me" (Chris Christian)

**Billy Larkin**
From the "Uptown Country" Album
"Sunshine Lady" (Chris Christian)


**SINGLES**

"Darlin' (This Time Girl) - Robbie Patton
(Chris Christian, Robbie Patton)

"Darlin" – Darryl Cotton                              # 1 in Australia
(Chris Christian, Robbie Patton)

"I Want You, I Need You" – Chris Christian            # 6 Billboard A/C
(Chris Christian, J. C. Crowley)                      #37 Billboard Top 100

"I Want You Back in my Life Again" – The Carpenters   #14 Billboard A/C
(Chris Christian, Kerry Chater)                       #72 Billboard Top 100

"Don't Worry Baby" – B J Thomas                       # 2 Billboard A/C
(Brian Wilson, Roger Christian)                       #17 Billboard Top 100
                                                      # 1 Canada RPM Adult Contemporary

"I Go To Pieces (Cotton, Lloyd & Christian)           #66  Billboard Top 100
(Del Shannon)                                         #10  Billboard A/C chart

"I Can Sing, I Can Dance" (Cotton, Lloyd & Christian) #19  Billboard A/C

"Home Where I Belong" – B J Thomas                    #98  Billboard Country
(Pat Terry)                                           #21  US Christian CHR

"Still the Lovin's Been Fun" – B J Thomas             # 8  Billboard A/C
(Chris Christian)                                     #77  Billboard Top 100

"God Bless The Children" – B J Thomas                 #38  Billboard A/C
(Chris Christian, Shanon Smith)

"Walkin' on a Cloud" – B J Thomas                     #30  Billboard A/C
(Chris Christian)

"Everything Always Works Out for the Best"            #10  US Christian CHR
(Chris Christian, Lewis Anderson)


A Grandmother's Prayer                                              227

HOME SWEET HOME RECORDS

## NUMBER ONE NATIONAL HITS

| Title | | Chart Position |
|---|---|---|
| IF YOU WERE THE ONLY ONE | Steve Archer w/The Archers | #1** |
| PRAISE THE LORD | Luke Garrett | #1** |
| THE ME NOBODY KNOWS | Marilyn McCoo | #1** |
| THE ANSWER | Eric Champion | #1** |
| JERUSALEM | Whiteheart | #1** |
| EVERMORE | Steve Archer/Debbie Boone | #1** |
| PUT YOUR TRUST | Chris Christian | #1** |
| STRONGER THAN THE WEIGHT | David Martin | #1** |
| HOLY IS OUR GOD | Michael James Murphy | #1** |
| WHAT YOU'RE LOOKING FOR | Eric Champion | #1** |
| THROUGH HIS EYES OF LOVE | Steve Archer | #1** |
| SAFE | Steve Archer/Marilyn McCoo | #1** |
| EVERYTHING I AM | Steve Archer | #1** |
| BUT YOU DIDN'T | Steve Archer | #1** |
| FOREVER LOVE | Eric Champion | #1** |
| BUFFALO CREEK | Dogwood | #1** |
| WHY DOES THE DEVIL HAVE ALL THE GOOD MUSIC | Chris Christian | #1** |
| MOUNTAIN TOP | Chris Christian | #1** |
| SAIL ON | Chris Christian and Imperials | #1** |
| PRAY AWAY | Chris Christian | #1** |
| LOVE THEM WHILE WE CAN | Chris Christian | #1** |
| PUT YOUR TRUST | Chris Christian | #1** |
| HOLY IS OUR GOD | Michael James Murphy | #1** |
| GET BACK TO THE BIBLE | Chris Christian | #1** |
| HEED THE CALL | Chris Christian and Imperials | #1** |
| LOVE DID IT AGAIN | Chris Christian | #1** |
| ARISE | Luke Garrett | #1** |
| A LIVING FIRE | Glenn Allen Green | #1** |
| DAY LIKE TODAY | Chris Christian w/Gerry Beckley | #1** |
| ALL THINGS ARE POSSIBLE | Dan Peek w/Chris Christian | #1** |
| HEAVEN MUST HAVE SENT YOU | Rick Riso | #1** |
| MAGNIFY | Luke Garrett | #1** |
| WE ARE HIS HANDS | Whiteheart w/Dann Huff, Amy Grant, Chris Christian | #1** |
| JERUSALEM | Whiteheart w/Dann Huff | #1** |
| HE'S RETURNING | Whiteheart | #1** |
| VITAL SIGNS | Whiteheart w/Dann Huff | #1** |
| HOTLINE | Whiteheart | #1** |
| CARRIED AWAY | Whiteheart w/Dann Huff | #1** |
| LET THE WIND BLOW | David Martin | #1** |
| CASTAWAY | Mark Heard | #1** |
| THE ANSWER | Eric Champion | #1** |

## TOP TEN NATIONAL HITS

| Song | Artist | Chart Position |
|---|---|---|
| MIRROR OF YOUR HEART | Chris Christian | Top 10* |
| WARRIOR FOR THE LORD | Marilyn McCoo | Top 10* |
| NOW I SEE THE MAN | Chris Christian | Top 10* |
| WITH YOUR LOVE | Chris Christian | Top 10* |
| MIRROR OF YOUR HEART | Chris Christian | Top 10* |
| EYE OF THE STORM | Mark Heard | Top 10* |
| I'LL DO MY BEST | Steve Archer | Top 10* |
| WINDS OF TIME | Mark Heard | Top 10* |
| PRAISE THE LORD | Chris Christian | Top 10* |
| LIVING SACRIFICE | Chris Christian | Top 10* |
| WE ARE AN OFFERING | Chris Christian | Top 10* |
| DOER OF THE WORD | Dan Peek | Top 10* |
| GOTTA HAVE THE REAL THING | Rick Riso | Top 10* |
| FOCUS ON THE CHILD | Chris Christian | Top 10* |
| JUDGEMENT IN THE GATE | Luke Garrett | Top 10* |
| I PUT MY HOPE | Gabriel | Top 10* |
| A SIMPLE PRAYER | Gabriel | Top 10* |
| HOLD ON | Whiteheart w/ Dann Huff | Top 10* |
| IN HIS NAME | Whiteheart | Top 10* |
| TAKE HIM TO HEART | David Martin | Top 10* |
| ALWAYS HERE | Eric Champion | Top 10* |
| REMEMBER ME | Rick Riso | Top 10* |
| I WANT YOU , I NEED YOU | Chris Christian w/Cheryl Ladd | Top 10* |

## TOP FORTY NATIONAL HITS

| Title | Artist | Chart Position |
|---|---|---|
| PART OF THE HEART | Steve Archer | Top 40 |
| SING UNTO THE LAMB | Whiteheart | Top 40 |
| SATISFACTION GUARANTEED | Chris Christian | Top 40 |
| FROM THE START | Chris Christian | Top 40 |
| FEELING OF YOUR LOVE | Chris Christian | Top 40 |
| SAVE THE WORLD | Eric Champion | Top 40 |
| (DON'T BLAME IT ON) THE ONES YOU LOVE | Chris Christian w/Bruce Carroll | Top 40 |
| CARRY ON | Whiteheart w/Steve Green | Top 40 |
| ASHES TO EMBERS | Dogwood | Top 40 |
| FROM THE START | Chris Christian | Top 40 |
| ALREADY LIVIN' IN HEAVEN | Chris Christian | Top 40 |
| TOO HEAVENLY MINDED | Chris Christian w/Steve Green | Top 40 |
| GIVE UP YOURSELF | Chris Christian | Top 40 |
| WEIGHT OF THE WORLD | Chris Christian | Top 40 |
| LIGHT AT THE END OF THE DARKNESS | Chris Christian w/ Larry Gatlin | Top 40 |
| NOBODY | Chris Christian w/ Andre Crouch | Top 40 |
| THE MAN BEHIND THE MAN | Chris Christian w/Gerry Beckley | Top 40 |
| THE FAITH THAT COMES FROM YOU | Chris Christian | Top 40 |
| DAKOTA'S THEME | Chris Christian | Top 40 |
| EVER CONSTANT | Chris Christian | Top 40 |
| EVER SURE | Rick Riso | Top 40 |
| WRITTEN ON MY HEART | Tami Gunden | Top 40 |
| CIRCLE OF GIVING | Luke Garrett | Top 40 |
| IN MAJESTY | Luke Garrett | Top 40 |
| HEART OF HEARTS | Mark Heard | Top 40 |
| AS IF WERE THE ONLY ONE TO LOVE | Luke Garrett | Top 40 |
| I LOVE YOU STILL | Chris Christian | Top 40 |
| NO KIDNAP TODAY | Michael James Murphy | Top 40 |
| MY MIND FORGETS A MILLION THINGS | Tami Gunden | Top 40 |
| THE WINDS OF TIME | Mark Heard | Top 40 |
| KEEP THE LOVELIGHT BURNING | Marilyn McCoo w/Billy Davis Jr. | Top 40 |
| ADONAI | David Martin | Top 40 |
| EVERYTHING | Dan Peek | Top 40 |
| YOUR FATHER LOVES YOU | Dan Peek | Top 40 |
| DIVINE LADY | Dan Peek | Top 40 |
| LOVE WAS JUST ANOTHER WORD | Dan Peek (with America) | Top 40 |
| FAITHFUL | Rick Riso | Top 40 |
| SURE THING | Rick Riso | Top 40 |
| SENDING OUT A PRAYER | Jeff Smith | Top 40 |
| EVERYDAY | Whiteheart w / Sandi Patti | Top 40 |
| NOTHING CAN TAKE THIS LOVE | Whiteheart w/ Dann Huff | Top 40 |
| QUIET LOVE | Whiteheart w/ Dann Huff | Top 40 |
| LET YOUR FIRST THOUGHT BE LOVE | Whiteheart w/ Dann Huff | Top 40 |

## CHRISTMAS NATIONAL HITS

| Title | Artist | Played Nationally each year |
|---|---|---|
| ON THIS CHRISTMAS NIGHT | B J Thomas | |
| BETHLEHEM MORNING | Steve Archer | |
| CHRISTMAS ALL YEAR 'ROUND | Chris Christian /Charlene | |
| GIFT OF LOVE | The Boones | |
| GLORIA | Whiteheart | |
| GOD BLESS THE CHILDREN | B J Thomas | |
| ALMOST CHRISTMASTIME | David Meece | |
| SANTA'S REINDEER RIDE | Amy Grant | |
| A SPECIAL WISH | B W Stevenson | |
| BORN A CHILD IN BETHLEHEM | Tennesse Ernie Ford | |
| GLORIA | Whiteheart | |
| WHO IS THIS ONE | Whiteheart | |
| CHRISTMAS KIND OF WORLD | Eric Champion | |
| HOSANNA | Whiteheart | |
| THINKING OF YOU THIS CHRISTMAS | Chris Christian | |
| CHRISTMAS WITH CHILDREN | Chris Christian | |

Key: ** = #1 Hit    * = Top 10 Hit
Source:   Christian Research Report
Contemporary Christian Music Magazine
Gospel Trade
Billboard

**MAJOR SPORT EVENTS ON NATIONAL TV**

1989  The NFL Today
1990  CBS This Morning
1990  U.S. Open  (Tennis)
1990  NCAA Football (CBS)
1990  Masters  (Golf)
1991  Masters  (Golf)
1991  U.S. Open  (Tennis)
1992  Masters  (Golf)
1992  The NFL Today
1992  PGA Championships (Golf)
1992  NCAA Basketball Tournament
1991  U.S. Open  (Tennis)
1993  U.S. Open  (Golf)
1993  U.S. Open  (Tennis)
1993  NCAA Basketball Tournament
1993  NFL Pre-Game

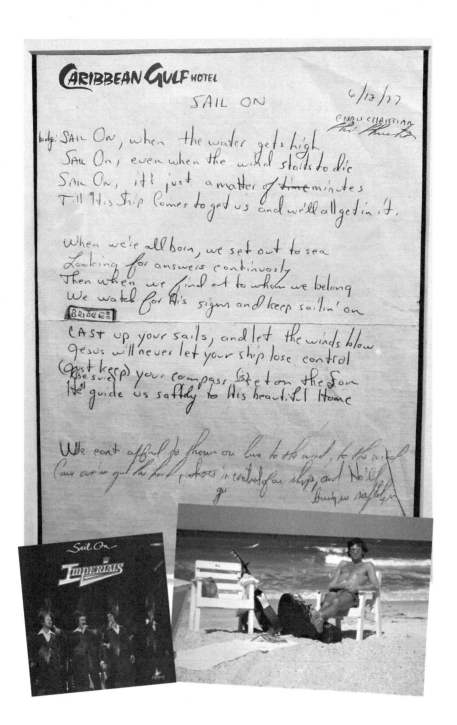

# CARIBBEAN GULF HOTEL

## SAIL ON

6/13/77

CHRIS CHRISTIAN
Phil Christ

bdg: SAIL On, when the water gets high
SAIL On, even when the wind starts to die
SAIL On, it's just a matter of ~~time~~ minutes
Till His Ship Comes to get us and we'll all get in it.

When we're all born, we set out to sea
Looking for answers continuosly
Then when we find out to whom we belong
We watch for His signs and keep sailin' on

BRIDGE:

CAST up your sails, and let the winds blow
Jesus will never let your ship lose control
(Just keep) your compass, (& set on the Son
(Be sure
He'll guide us safely to His beautiful Home

We can't afford to throw our lives to the wind, to the wind
Cuz we've got the Lord, who's in control of our ship, and He'll
g²
Bring us safely in

A Grandmother's Prayer

# CHRISTMAS IN NEW YORK

Nathan East
Chris Christmas

*[handwritten: Thank you Ruth Pointer 2005]*

*[handwritten: What a Great Song to Sing Love Anit. Pointer]*

### VS. 1
STROLLIN DOWN 5$^{TH}$ AVENUE
GOT SOME WINDOW SHOPPING LEFT TO DO
ROCKERFELLER AND BROADWAY
WHAT A PLACE TO SPEND A CHRISTMAS HOLIDAY

### VS. B  THERE'S A SPIRIT IN THE AIR,
EVERYWHERE

*[handwritten: Love the Groove Issa Pointer]*

### CHORUS:
THERE AIN'T NOTHING LIKE CHRISTMAS IN NEW YORK
TAKE A HORSE AND CARRIAGE RIDE AROUND THE PARK
ROUND THE WORLD, THERE IS CHRISTMAS IN THE HEART
BUT THERE AIN'T NOTHING LIKE CHRISTMAS IN NEW YORK

### VS. 2

TAKE A TAXI TO TIME SQUARE
SNOW IS FALLING ON NEON EVERYWHERE
THERE IS NO PLACE I'D RATHER BE
THAN IN THE APPLE ON ROCKIN' NEW YEARS EVE
*[handwritten: WHAT]*
IT'S A TIME EVERYONE CAN CELEBRATE,  CELEBRATE
*[handwritten: IT'S A PLACE WHERE WE CAN CELEBRATE]*
*[handwritten: WHAT A RACE TO SPEND the HOLIDAY — Bring the family and]*
THE BROADWAY LIGHTS
FORTY SECOND NEVER SHINED TO BRIGHT
TAKE A TAXI TO TIME SQUARE
SNOW IS FALLING, ON NEON EVERYWHERE
IT'S A TIME EVERYONE CAN CELEBRATE, CELEBRATE

*[handwritten: From every.]*

### VS. B

*[handwritten: What a place to spend the holiday From every corner of the world - people come and celebrate]*

*Pat Boone*

July 10, 1972

Mr. Chris Smith
c/o Archie Campbell
Route 3, Meadow Lake
Brentwood, Tennessee

Hi Chris!

I don't see a date on your letter, but I have a feeling it's been here for a couple of weeks. I'm sorry for the delay - but my whole life currently seems like a series of sits and starts, rushes and delays.

I'm thrilled to know that Jeannie C. Riley had read our book and given you a copy. I'm thanking God for the "shock waves" that seem to be spreading through the music and entertainment business these days. I should have known that God wouldn't leave out singers and musicians in His plan for the last days!

Yes, I know your song, "Thank You", and it is in the stack of songs for our next Jesus Music album. I realize it gets tedious and patience testing for a song writer, waiting for something to happen with his music. But I'm glad that you have reminded us about it, and all I can do at this moment is just assure you that we intend for it to be in our next session. Its been slow going, because MGM has not shown any enthusiasm for hymns or Jesus Music - therefore a "completed Jewish" brother and I have started a Jesus record company called "Lamb and Lion". We'll have MGM distribution, but not be tied exclusively to them. God is moving, and I just want you to be brought up to date on what's happening record wise. I pray that you'll be hearing a Pat Boone record of your song on Lamb and Lion before much longer.

God bless you, Chris, and use you there in the Nashville area where its been so tough for God to really break through the religious "crust" so prevelant there. He wants to do mighty things in Nashville and with all those good folks - but He has to be in control, not them!

I'll be gone the whole month of August and into September on tour, but if you stay in touch with my folks, I'm hoping to zoom in there privately for a few days in August. Maybe we can meet then.

The Caprenter's helper,

PAT BOONE

PB:jef

9255 SUNSET BOULEVARD / SUITE 706 / LOS ANGELES, CALIFORNIA 90069 / (213) 274-0751

A Grandmother's Prayer

Dear Chris,                                    8/19/72

J.E. ate dinner with us today and told us about your telephone call last night. Bless you! I wish you were through with college degree and draft board so you could take up these opportunities. But with your talent, hard work, etc. they will come again. I guess, then the fear of being drafted will cause you to get that degree which, this day + time, is so essential in any field. Power to our first grandchild!! We are ~~so proud of you~~! God is answering our prayers, and will for other grand-children if only they will do their ~~part~~ as you are doing. Prov. 10:4; 13:4,11. God rewards the diligent, not the slothful.

                    Love You!
                    Grand Tida

Mark Heard
% Familie von Lerber
Letzistrasse 14
8006 Zurich
Switzerland

May 4, 1981

Chris & Shanon Christian
Beverly Hills, California  90210

Dear Chris,

Officially,  THANKS!

Sincerely,

Mark

Mark

P.S. Keep in touch.

FINGERPRINT COMMUNICATIONS

P.O. BOX 834 MONTROSE, CALIFORNIA 91020 U.S.A.

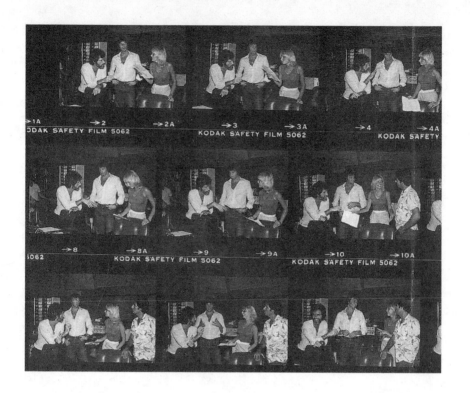

FRIDAY, MARCH 6, 2015

## #61 ALL THINGS ARE POSSIBLE by Dan Peek (1978)

ALL THINGS ARE POSSIBLE by Dan Peek (1978)

*All Things Are Possible* was #1 on the Christian Charts for weeks and Top 10 on the Billboard A/C charts. The album missed out on winning a **Grammy** when the award went to the **Imperials'** *Heed the Call* instead...also produced by **Chris Christian**.

One song on the album turned out to be historic -- the last time that Peek would ever record with both of his former **America** bandmates with a song written by **Chris Christian** and **Steve Kipner**.

**Chris Christian** was responsible for this collaboration between the original members of **America**. "I called Gerry and said, 'Hey, would you and Dewey come over here and sing on this Christian record for Dan?' He and Dewey agreed. There was not any animosity – at least, not any apparent negative exchanges. I think that's the last time the three guys sang together."

A Grandmother's Prayer

**#291 LET THE MUSIC START by Chris Christian (1984)**

LET THE MUSIC START by Chris Christian (1984)
Myrrh Records - SPCN 7-01-679906-9

## Producer: **Chris Christian**

Time Capsule-Worthy Track:
*Clap Your Hands*

Other Standout Tracks:
*Every Good and Perfect Gift*
*We Are An Offering*
*Sing With Joy*

**Chris Christian** always seemed to be in the right place at the right time.

He was born **Lon Christian Smith** in 1951 in Abilene, Texas. After attending Abilene Christian College, he headed for Nashville with $100 in his pocket. He started performing at the **Opryland** amusement park, met a few notables in the music industry, and ended up writing a song that would be recorded by none other than **Elvis Presley**. Stories like that were possible back in those days. From there, he became part of the group **Cotton, Lloyd and Christian**, then an artist in his own right, as well as a sought-after producer. He not only discovered **Amy Grant**, he also practically *invented* the soft-rock CCM sound that became so pervasive in the late 70s and beyond. In the Seventies, Christian was instrumental in either launching or helping to sustain the careers of many artists, including **B.J. Thomas, The Imperials, Dogwood, Fireworks, Dan Peek**, and many others. His songs were recorded by many secular performers as well.

Fast-forward to the Eighties. Christian was still very busy writing songs and producing albums for the likes of **Mark Heard, White Heart, Steve Archer, Olivia Newton-John, Hall and Oates, Natalie Cole, The Pointer Sisters, The Carpenters, Dionne Warwick, Donnie Osmond**, and many more. His musical instincts were always right in line with what was popular on Top 40 radio in any given year. But in '84 there was a new sound brewing...a fresh wind of the Spirit blowing.

First, let's back up just a bit.

Before the 1970s, our idea of "praise and worship" consisted almost exclusively of congregants singing in churches from hymnals. Slowly, that began to change. First, **Maranatha! Music** released a string of "praise" albums in the 70s and early 80s. Then **Keith Green's** *Songs For The Shepherd* and Phil Driscoll's *Sound the Trumpet* were widely regarded as "praise" albums in 1982.

By 1984, the trickle of praise became a flowing river of worship.

Driscoll's *I Exalt Thee* and **Kelly Willard's** *Psalms, Hymns and Spiritual Songs* moved decidedly toward reverence and awe. But a "recovering" CCM artist by the name of **Terry Clark** can truly be credited (although he would want no credit) with devising a new way for the body of Christ to worship God. His *Living Worship* and *Let's Worship* albums, in '84 and '86 respectively, allowed us to first eavesdrop on, and then participate in a musical conversation with Jesus...which led to authentic spiritual intimacy and transparency before the Lord. These were deeper waters.

And then, there was *Let The Music Start*, also recorded in 1984 by **Chris Christian**, a member of the "CCM establishment" if there ever was one. He was certainly not known as a worship artist, but in '84 **Chris Christian** joined Clark, Willard and Driscoll in predicting a trend, not following one. After all, these "worship" albums were released long before "worship" became a genre...long before worship music dominated the airwaves of Christian radio stations...and well before a modern worship revival swept through America and the U.K.

"It was quite a unique kind of album at the time of release," agreed songwriter **Dwight Liles**, who penned several songs on the record. "The thing that made *Let The Music Start* even more unique was that the production values were almost totally synth-pop. There was simply no worship music being done in that up-to-the-minute, radio-friendly style at the time other than **Michael W. Smith's** hit, *Great Is The Lord* and some of **Twila Paris'** early worship songs."

Indeed, **Chris Christian** brought the same soothing, radio-friendly production values to this "vintage" praise album that he did to all of his other records. Keyboards were dominating most soft rock and pop music of that era; they were capably handled here by **Keith Thomas, Mark Gersmehl** and Christian himself. **Gary Lunn** and **Jimmie Lee Sloas** (later of **The Imperials**) supplied the bottom end along with drummers **David Huff** and **Dennis Holt**. David's brother Dann played guitar, as did **Jon Goin**. The talented **Jack Joseph Puig** engineered the album with help from **Jeff Balding**.

The record kicks off with *Clap Your Hands*. If you were a Christian in your teens or twenties in 1984, you probably saw the memorable video for this track on *TBN's Real Videos*. From a video production standpoint, it's Eighties all the way, complete with shots of **Chris Christian** "playing" a keyboard scarf on the beach and inserting a cassette of his own album in his car's tape player. If you were a stickler for realism, you were probably bothered by the fact that Christian was playing a Kawai acoustic grand piano over what should have obviously been a synthesizer during the "recording studio" scene. But hey...creative license, right?

Musically, *Clap Your Hands* would've felt right at home on a **Sandi Patty** or **Larnelle Harris** album. It's also somewhat reminiscent of the aforementioned *Great Is The Lord* by **Michael W. Smith**. Lyrically, it set the tone for what was to follow.

Some "wonderfully 80s" keyboard parts get us into *Lift Up His Name*, a song that prescribes praise as the key to discovering true love, lasting peace and joy.

*Blessed Be the Lord* sounds like something early **White Heart** might've recorded, with lyrics that seem to be taken mostly from Scripture.

*Every Good and Perfect Gift* is a smooth, pop-oriented repackaging of James 1:17. It's one of the record's more memorable tracks, with a hook that stays with you.

*We Are An Offering*, an inspirational ballad written by **Dwight Liles,** closes out Side One and definitely moves away from praise and toward worship. It has a hymn-like quality and expresses total devotion to the Lord.

"I wrote *We Are An Offering* and *Clap Your Hands* on the same day, May 12, 1983," songwriter **Dwight Liles** revealed. "I had gone over to my parents' house that morning specifically to do some songwriting on my mother's upright piano. I had just finished writing *Clap Your Hands* and was still feeling creative when I looked through my title list, and decided to work on one of the titles there, *We Are An Offering*."

Liles continued: "Once I started playing some chords, the words and melody just seemed to 'fall from heaven,' and I literally came up with the entire song in the time it takes to sing it. I stopped and scribbled down the words as they came to me. It is probably the one song I ever wrote that I can say came to me entirely without effort on my part. It was as if I were taking dictation."

Songwriter **Dwight Liles**

*Sing With Joy* is a celebration of praise, with lyrics that sound very much like they could've been penned by King David himself. It's another song that was written by **Dwight Liles.**

"*Sing With Joy* was co-written with **Niles Borop,**" Liles said. "We didn't write it specifically for this project. **Chris Christian** was my publisher at the time, and he received worktapes and lyrics of all my songs, so he selected them because he considered them appropriate for what he was doing. The phrase 'let the music start' is from the first verse of *Sing With Joy*, so you could say that *Sing With Joy* is the 'title track' of the album in the sense that the lyric of that song provided Chris with the idea for the album's title."

Musically, *Sing With Joy* has a 'Smitty" vibe (as in Michael W.).

*With the Name of Jesus* is a bit of a departure -- the only track on the album that isn't technically a praise or worship song. It's a bouncy pop track that serves as an exhortation to fellow believers regarding the power that is found in the name above all names. Like many of the record's other tracks, this song borrows much from the words of Scripture. And that's a good thing.

On *Oh Magnify The Lord*, Christian takes a praise chorus that was popular in charismatic church circles at that time and transforms it into a 80s pop tune. Like almost every track on **Let the Music Start**, this one is drenched in synthesizers. No complaints here.

Early **White Heart** lineup. Yeah, that's **Steve Green**, 2nd from the left...

*Make A Joyful Noise* continues much in the same vein, musically and lyrically, as the rest of the album. This one is definitely reminiscent of early **White Heart**...probably because the group actually performs with Chris on this track.

In the Scriptures, the word *selah* occurred frequently at the end of a verse in Psalms and Habakkuk, probably as a musical direction (or so scholars say). A short instrumental by that same name wraps up **Let the Music Start**. It's about 90 seconds long, and there's an interesting story that goes with it.

"While Chris was recording the project," recalled **Dwight Liles**, "he let me hear another song of mine and **Niles Borop's** that he had recorded for the album called *Immortal Invisible* (not to be confused with the classic hymn of the same title). The track had a very, very long fade. I didn't like what he had done with the song. We'd written it as a mid-tempo hymn, and he'd recorded it as an uptempo synth-pop piece. Of course, I didn't complain to Chris about that. But as it turned out, Chris chose not to include the song on the album. Instead, he clipped off the long fade-out, and that section became *Selah*.

So, there you have it...an early entry in the worship catalog from an unlikely artist. One reviewer described this album as "the perfect companion when you are seeking to reflect and meditate on simple Biblical truths and promises."

We cannot overlook the oversized role he played in developing and packaging what came to be known as "contemporary Christian music."

Appendix

So, it has been quite a ride, a very full and diverse career for the guy with the funny name from Abilene. But he had his finger on the pulse of what God was saying to His church in 1984. And there's a record to prove it.

From the album's liner notes:

*"It is my desire that the melodies and words of these songs will find their way to the worship times of bodies of believers around the world; and that the praises, and ideas that they offer, live far beyond this record. Sing along with joy."*

-Chris Christian

blog by Scott Bachmann

A Grandmother's Prayer

# Thank you, Chris. Thank you, very much.

 **Abilene Reporter News**
PART OF THE USA TODAY NETWORK

Elvis trumps all.

These days, people will want to read something political into that choice of verbs.
But this is not fake news: If you have a connection to The King, you rock.
And roll, too.

I talked last week to Chris Christian, a familiar name for years but someone I never
have met. I thought and thought about a song I heard on the radio growing up and
finally, the remake of "I Go to Pieces," when the Abilene singer was a member of
Cotton, Lloyd and Christian, came back to me.

I heard it on the radio in 1975 when I was a high school junior.

In 1981, as a solo artist, Chris cracked the Top 40 with "I Want You, I Need You." It
was a Top 10 adult contemporary hit.

Chris has been a great success in many areas in his life, including landing some hits
in the Top 40. But it's his connection to Elvis that not only is a great Abilene story but
one that may bring a crowd to 609 Scott Place this weekend.

After all, it's where he wrote a song that The King recorded in 1973 and was
released on Jan. 8, 1975 — why is that date special, Elvis fans?

It was his 40th birthday.

"Love Song of the Year" is Track 5.

Chris' parents now are deceased and an estate sale of the J.E. Smith home is
planned. A few music items of interest will be available, including signed copies of
Chris' albums.

But what really is cool is that as a junior at Abilene High in 1968, he wrote a song
titled "Love Song of the Year." Something he did when he wasn't playing basketball
and being a high school kid almost ready to get on with life.

A song written by a high school student in Abilene sung by The King. Is America the
land of opportunity, or what?

Before the story of Chris Christian Smith (and you thought he used "Christian" just to
score points ...) going to Nashville to seek fame and fortune, there's the story of his
fourth-grade teacher bringing a musician to class one day.

His teacher at Crockett Elementary was Mrs. (Helen) Patterson. One day, her son
Dow visited the class. He talked to the kids about writing and performing songs. One
of his songs was getting some radio airplay.

He was a celebrity.

"I thought, 'Gee, that's what I want to do,'" Chris said.

**At 609 Scott Place in east Abilene, Chris Christian Smith, then an Abilene High junior in 1968, wrote
"Love Song of the Year," which Elvis later recorded.**

But, you know, that's just a kid's impossible dream. Like hitting a home run in the
bottom of the 9th to win the World Series. And the crowd goes wild!

Appendix

"To come from Abilene to Nashville and Elvis record one of your songs?" Chris said, laughing. Never happen.

But it did, thanks to Shaun Nielsen singing his friend's song one early morning to Elvis, who obviously remembered that song when he woke up later in the day.

All this was just three months or so after Chris, now an Abilene Christian University graduate and whose grandfather served as vice president under 29-year president Don Morris, packed his bags and drove to Nashville.

Even Tony Brown, the well-known producer for Reba McEntire, Vince Gill, George Strait and others quickly is linked to The King. Despite dozens of No. 1 hits by those stars, Brown is remembered for playing the piano for Elvis until his death in 1977.

Chris is doing a documentary on Brown and the musician-producer commented that people often are more interested in his time with The King than his success producing country music.

"Elvis defines us," Chris said. You almost could hear him shaking his head but grinning on the phone.

Chris is not sure but he may be the youngest songwriter whose work Elvis recorded.

Now, through the years, many other artists recorded his work, including Olivia Newton-John and B.J. Thomas. Even the Carpenters and the Pointer Sisters, certainly two diverse acts involving siblings.

Chris Christian, right, performs as a member of Cotton, Lloyd and Christian on the TV music show "Midnight Special."

But that one song ...

A comment on the YouTube is: *"Love it.........forever Elvis..."*

Chris also posted.

*"I wrote this song when I was in High School."* Chris Christian @ccsongwriter

And here's more irony. He signed Amy Grant, who is in Abilene on Thursday to tour the West Texas Rehabilitation Center and then perform at its summer dinner show.

One story you may hear is Chris getting her a gig for $500.

But, Mr. Christian, she supposedly said, ... I don't have $500.

No, Amy, they will pay *you* $500.

Chris has quite the resumé, in addition to the performing and recording days, that also included success in Christian music.

He produced and did music for the well-known Gerbert children's show.

He has been nominated for many Grammy and Dove Awards, winning nine times.

He started his own label, Sweet Home Records.

He once purchased The Studios at Las Colinas.

He was CEO of World Digital Media Group.

Today, he is vice chairman of the Dallas Wings, the WNBA franchise.

From left: Dick Clark, Robert Kardashian and Chris Christian in the early 1980s. Christian performed on Clark's "American Bandstand" in 1982.

A Grandmother's Prayer

Yep, the Abilene boy has done pretty good for himself. Lots of memories of days with that fluffed, blow-dried 1970s-80s hair and rolled up suit sleeves. Performing on "American Bandstand."

On that 1982 show, host Dick Clark said what baffled him about the multi-talented Chris was why he didn't just take a plush office job instead of returning to music.
"Well, uh, I think music is something I've always loved so much," Chris responded. He did get around to that office job.
Chris along the way probably met everyone who was anyone in the music business. But writing Track 5 on the "Promised Land" ... Tony Brown understands.
Some folks may show up this weekend just to see the house where one of Elvis' songs was written. They might get all shook up.
Chris may have left the building, but the Elvis history has not.

*Greg Jaklewicz*
*Abilene Reporter News*

Appendix

### CHRIS CHRISTIAN

Chris Christian began his music career in 1974 as a performer based in Nashville. Chris is a songwriter, a publishing and record company executive a record producer best known for starting the career of Amy Grant and writing for Elvis Presley. He has produced albums that were nominated for 8 Grammy Awards, winning 4. He has also been nominated for 7 Gospel Music Dove Awards winning 5. Chris started Home Sweet Home Records in 1981 in Nashville and released 65 albums that included B.J. Thomas. At one time Chris played guitar in the Chet Atkins band. In 1992 he acquired the studios in Las Colinas in Irving, Texas. He is also an owner of the WNBA team, Dallas Wings.

Chris Christian qualified for the West Texas Music Hall of Fame Honor Roll by having a single, "I Want You, I Need You" that reached #37 in the Pop Charts in 1981. He was inducted into The Christian Music Hall of Fame in 2007. Chris Christian was born in Abilene, Texas.

West Texas Music Hall of Fame

Please visit www.grandmothersprayer.com for additional resources, more images, the backstory behind the color images in this book, and to share your "Grandmother's Prayer" story.